India-EU Free Trade Agreement

Conflict and Human Rights Studies Network

Conflict and Human Rights Studies Network, Manipur is a network initiated in 2012 by academicians and scholars dedicated to the study of conflict originating from armed struggle and others, and related human rights issues in the North east India. The network strives to fill-up the gap between academicians and human rights activists to bring about peaceful resolution to the ongoing armed-conflict in the region.

About the Authors

Homen Thangjam is Assistant Professor of Political Science, the Maharaja Bodhchandra College, Imphal. He received his doctoral degree from Jawaharlal Nehru University, New Delhi and specializes in Democratization Theories and Conflict Transformation. He can be reached at <homenth@gmail.com>.

Hanjabam Ishworchandra Sharma is Assistant Professor of Economics, Manipur University. He received his doctoral degree from Manipur University, Canchipur and specializes in Agriculture Economics. He can be reached at <isworhanja@gmail.com>

Shukhdeba Sharma Hanjabam is Assistant Professor of Social Work, Indira Gandhi National Tribal University, Regional-Campus, Manipur. He received his doctoral degree from Tata Institute of Social Sciences, Mumbai and specializes in human rights and conflict transformation especially in the context of the North East India. He can be reached at <hanjabam@gmail.com>.

India-EU
Free Trade Agreement
Potential Impact on the Northeast India

Homen Thangjam
Hanjabam Isworchandra Sharma
Shukhdeba Sharma Hanjabam

Published for
Conflict and Human Rights Studies Network, Manipur
by
CONCEPT PUBLISHING COMPANY PVT. LTD.
NEW DELHI-110059

ISBN-13: 978-93-5125-148-4

First Published 2017

Published and Printed by

Concept
Since 1974

Concept Publishing Company Pvt. Ltd.
Regd. Office:
A/15-16, Commercial Block, Mohan Garden,
New Delhi-110059 (INDIA)
Phones : 25351460, 25351794, *Fax* : 091-11-25357109
Email : publishing@conceptpub.com
Website: www.conceptpub.com

Cataloging in Publication Data—DK Courtesy: D.K. Agencies (P) Ltd. <docinfo@dkagencies.com>

Thangjam, Homen, author.
India-EU free trade agreement : potential impact on the Northeast India / Homen Thangjam, Hanjabam Isworchandra Sharma, Shukhdeba Sharma Hanjabam.
pages cm
Includes bibliographical references and index.
ISBN 9789351251484

1. Free trade—India. 2. Free trade—European Union countries. 3. India—Commerce—European Union countries. 4. European Union countries—Commerce—India. 5. Manipur (India)—Commercial policy. I. Sharma, Hanjabam Isworchandra, author. II. Hanjabam, Shukhdeba Sharma, 1983- author. III. Conflict and Human Rights Studies Network (Manipur, India), publisher. IV. Title.

HF2323.I53 2017 DDC 382.95404 23

Preface

Starting from the 1990s, the North eastern part of India became an extremely important strategic area for the policy-makers in New Delhi. For example, policy-makers in order to make a foray into the domain of South East Asia and East Asia initiated what is today known as the Look East Policy so as to forge a greater economic and strategic tie with Association for South East Asian Nations (ASEAN). Although a byproduct of post-Cold War geo-political reconfigurations, the significance and necessity of the policy could be seen as a foreign policy response on the part of India. Also, such developments provided the grounds for opening up of India's economy to global capitalism. Other than signing Regional Trade Agreement (RTA) with the ASEAN in 1990, other RTAs that have potential impact on the North east include agreements undertaken with countries such as Thailand and Singapore. Negotiations having similar interest and ones that would potentially impinge upon the North east is underway with the BIMSTEC Group, China and Malaysia etc. The recent most case is the proposed India-EU Free Trade Agreement.

Two broad areas can be identified that have direct bearing on the people of the North east on account of such agreements. One relates with security *per se* (militarization) and the other is the issue of livelihood, although both terms can be included under the broad category of human security, and are intrinsically interrelated.

This study is divided into six chapters. First chapter deals with the available discourses on free trade and how it has found a formidable place in the neoliberal economic regime of today's world. In doing so, we have made an attempt to contextualize the setting of the present study. Second chapter focuses on the relationship between India and European Union, and the proposal for free trade agreement between the two. In the absence of a policy paper on the proposed agreement, the study relies on various other sources to have an understanding of the agreement.

Third chapter deals briefly with the economic position of Manipur, within it the rationale given by the Governments, both Central and State, to "invite" investment in the State so as to uplift its economic situation. It also highlights the human rights situation as well development experience including trade in the state which have invariably affected the indigenous population and resources.

Fourth chapter deals with mining and oil exploration and drilling. Two case studies on Odisha and Meghalaya are analysed as reference points for understanding the reality of mining in India, and the precaution that need to be developed in the case of Manipur. The case of Reliant Energy is also put forward in the study to underscore plight of the people in terms of resource conservation and livelihood issues. Fifth chapter deals with the issue of food security in Manipur.

The last chapter as a way of recommendation suggests for humane approach to trade agreement, especially the India-EU FTA, to safeguard human rights and rights of the indigenous people. Such suggestions underscore the fact that in the prevailing global neo-liberal economic system, it is simply impossible to prevent countries entering into trade agreements but a plea can always be made to incorporate policy and legal measures to protect human security of the indigenous people in terms of ownership of land and resources as well as the environment.

Methodology

The study was largely based on the analysis of data available in the public domain. For this study we have used both primary and secondary data. Perception about the prospect of the trade or its impact was also collected from stakeholders and interaction with project proponents, funders (e-mail interviews), lawyers, NGOs, media group, human rights defenders, traders, local weavers and artisans, policy-makers, academicians etc. were conducted. We also have used secondary information for this study. Documents from websites and contacts we set up. News paper clippings, books and other publications have been used.

Homen Thangjam
Hanjabam Isworchandra Sharma
Shukhdeba Sharma Hanjabam

Acknowledgements

We are grateful to Centre for Social Development, Imphal, particularly Urikhimbam Nobokishore (Secretary) and Takhenchangbam Chaoba Sharma (Coordinator) for supporting the study and also for proving platform for field interactions across northeast region and New Delhi.

Homen Thangjam
Hanjabam Isworchandra Sharma
Shukhdeba Sharma Hanjabam

Contents

List of Tables

List of Figures

List of Boxes

1

Free Trade

Setting the Context

Free trade refers to the unregulated exchange of raw materials, commodities, and services among people and nations. With the Cold War over, politicians, economists and others have been promoting unfettered free trade and free market ideology or neoliberalism, pushing it to an even wider international arena to facilitate international trade. Richard Robbins[1], summarizes some of the guiding principles of this ideology, which include:

- Sustained economic growth as the way to human progress;
- Free markets without government "interference" allow for the most efficient and socially optimal allocation of resources;
- Economic globalization is beneficial to everyone;
- Privatization removes inefficiencies of the public sector; and
- Governments should mainly function to provide the infrastructure to advance the rule of law with respect to property rights and contracts.

The assumptions that are made to support the neoliberalism ideology according to J.M. Blaut in "the colonizer's model of the world" include:

- Humans are motivated by self-interest, greed etc., expressed best through pursuit of financial gains;
- Actions that result in greatest financial gains benefit society the most;
- Competitive behaviour is more rational for individuals than cooperation, hence societies should be structured around this motive; and
- Progress is measured by increased materialistic consumption and so ever more consumption should be favoured.

The implementation of overly simplified theories and ideologies are meeting growing criticisms. For example, former chief economist of the World Bank Joseph Stiglitz, heavily criticizes the International Monetary Fund (IMF) for pursuing an ideology of neoliberal "market fundamentalism" which is overly simplistic, without paying attention to real human needs while also being influenced by, and meeting the needs of, the finance community.[2] At the same time, Stiglitz makes a great case for market economics, but without the ideology, recognizing the complexities, and the roles society and democracy must play.

The definition of progress and success is measured in material terms, and other concerns such as environmental issues, or human perspectives of emotional richness or social well-being, are not necessarily factored in. For example, different cultures also have a different meaning of progress and poverty. Exporting one culture's definition *via* such an ideology can risk causing societal problems if not done in an open and democratic way. Joseph Stiglitz is of the opinion that institutions such as the IMF and World Bank are not doing this in a very democratic way, even if it is claimed so.[3] Where the market has become so detached from society and does not meet its needs, this project is doomed for failure he suggests. Those cultures that realize the market works best when it is embedded in society will, if given the chance by the powerful countries, be likely to succeed. Environmental concerns are typically not taken into account of directly. It is argued that the environment will benefit indirectly because the same process of individual greed will create markets that address environmental problems. Yet, this creates *unnecessary jobs* (which also uses more resources) because sustainable development that would not have to adversely affect the environment in the first place would be a more efficient form of development.

Furthermore, and very importantly, those who are wealthier tend to wield more economic and political power and influence. Hence, leaders and elite of powerful nations or segments of society are more able to exert their influences, if needed. This can happen not only in places where rule of law and strong institutions are lacking, but also the most democratic of societies. In more developed economies, such influence can be subtle, or appear to be distant because it may not affect the local society as much as it does to people half way around the world. Hence, what can be promoted in the interest of some political and business elite, may not necessarily be the same as society's interests in general and it can also "distort" markets. Moreover, corporations have been given the rights that ordinary individuals have. This has allowed even more concentrated power and influence to be exerted.

The use of political influence includes using the military as well, if needed. Such use and abuse of power has been there throughout history. "Gun Boat Diplomacy" for example, was a common tactic by the British Empire to force open other countries to trade in terms favourable to the Empire. Military power has also contributed to the processes in the current forms of globalization as well.

Similar influences of power have given rise to disastrous policies of the International Monetary Fund (IMF) and World Bank, such as the Structural Adjustment Programmes (SAPs) that have forced poor countries to cut back on health and education expenditures. Such measures combined with the contentious rules of the World Trade Organization (WTO) form a backbone to today's globalization. As J.W. Smith of the Institute for Economic Democracy suggests, this maintains *unequal* rules of trade and, ultimately, continues to deepen inequality, poverty and exploitation.

Evolution of Free Trade

Adam Smith and Free Trade

One of the foundational propositions of economic theory since the seminal work of Adam Smith is that free trade is ultimately superior to protectionism if the principal economic objective is the greatest possible quantity of aggregate wealth or national income, and, indeed, the greatest good for all people.[4] The mercantilists composed their tracts during the seventeenth and eighteenth centuries, a period of tremendous colonial activity, trade growth, and, not coincidentally, nation-state formation. Mercantilists predictably celebrated foreign trade but also believed strongly in the need to protect national industries and markets. They supported a wide range of protectionist measures, including tariffs on imports and subsidies for exports. Among Smith's contributions was the theoretical refutation of the mercantilist argument for the promotion of exports and discouragement of imports, especially manufactured imports. Smith argued that the economy-wide impact of trade policies and regulations had to be examined. For instance, high duties on imports that were produced more cheaply elsewhere tended to diminish domestic competition and promote expansion of an inefficient industry. For example, protecting the British textile industry from cheaper colonial imports would lead to more investment of labour and resources in a demonstrably inefficient sector of the economy. Without protections, resources could be allocated to industries that were more competitive on the world market and which would thus realize greater economic aggregate growth, also known as static gains from trade.

Full analyses of the economic benefits of the division of labour and the public benefits of private self-interest were among Smith's foremost contributions to free trade economics. The rewards from the division of labour are implicit in his argument for static gains: "Nations that specialize in industries in which they are most competitive in unregulated conditions make the most efficient use of their labour and productive resources; thus both the specializing nations and the nations with which they trade will benefit."[5] In the long-term, these specialization-based static gains lead to dynamic gains; though dynamic gains are less clearly defined and more difficult to measure, they potentially accrue through the general economic impact of the more efficient use of resources.

Free Trade and Theory of Comparative Advantage

The powerful case for free trade submitted by Smith was made into prescriptive economic doctrine by the next generation of economists, who further developed what came to be labelled classical economics. David Ricardo, who is generally credited with the theory of comparative advantage — in short, the idea that even nations that lacked absolute advantage (producing goods at the least possible cost) could still realize gains by concentrating on production of goods of the greatest market competitiveness relative to other goods. James Mill developed the most comprehensive explanation of comparative advantage among the classical economists.

In response to a vigorous public debate regarding Britain's protectionist Corn Laws, Mill explained that protectionist tariffs led to an absolute economic loss. Taxes on imported corn led to increases in the price of corn in Britain, which in turn led to an increase in the cultivation of less-productive land, which in turn increased the value and rent costs of land, which finally led to necessary wage increases. Thus, in protecting an inefficient product, a widespread set of increased costs ensued, netting a general or absolute loss. Resources would have been far better and more naturally invested in sectors of the economy that did not need to be protected because they were already competitive, or, in other words, sectors in which national comparative advantage already existed.

The doctrine of comparative advantage did much to establish free trade as the ruling economic orthodoxy for several succeeding generations of economists and, until the arrival of the Great Depression and the British economist John Maynard Keynes, it ruled economic theory (if not quite practice) with little exception. Two exceptions that received the most vigorous debate were related to "infant industries" and national defence. The infant industries argument proposed that new industries deserved some form of government protection until they had the chance to establish themselves as competitors in the global market. While his assertion was vigorously disputed, the idea was effectively made practice (to no small success) by Alexander Hamilton in the early years of American national economic development. Also, in times of national emergency (e.g., war), interference in the workings of the free market was widely accepted as advisable. How, for instance, was supplying your enemy with goods for war to be justified? While wars may well be fought in the interests of the free market, the conditions and implications of war merit exception.

Free Trade vs. Market Intervention or the New Deal

Whatever the sideline debates among economists regarding the particular cases for suspending the rules of free trade, it took the work of Keynes to establish a rigorous and widely accepted critique of free trade doctrine. Keynes, with considerable theoretical sophistication, faced the facts of the catastrophic market failure that goes by the name of the Great Depression and demonstrated the need to pursue protectionist measures. His General Theory of Employment, Interest, and Money included arguments for government spending on public works and promoting public investment and consumption during periods of high unemployment.[6] Keynes did not believe that free market conditions realized, or "settled" at, full employment and that unemployment was a principal indicator of economic inefficiency. Government interventions in the market, including protective tariffs and subsidies, were, he asserted, sometimes necessary to restore employment and general economic health.

Keynes was enormously influential, not least in the United States, where his theories informed Franklin D. Roosevelt's massive government market intervention known as the New Deal. Towards the end of Second World War (1939–1945), Keynes was a key figure at the meeting in Bretton Woods, New Hampshire, where two institutions were created that would come to dominate international economic relations in the later decades of the twentieth century: the International Monetary Fund (IMF) and the World Bank. However, these organizations, chartered under the banner of free trade principles, did not become important institutions of global economic management until after the Cold War ended. Until the end of the Cold War, the global free market was effectively compromised by the manoeuvrings of the superpowers as they intervened in the economic affairs of nations according to their particular national and ideological interests.

GLOBAL ARTICULATION FOR FREE TRADE

Since the Cold War, the IMF and the World Bank, along with the World Trade Organization (WTO, established in 1995), have come to dominate the vigorous global articulation of free trade principles and practices. Throughout the Cold War, developing nations were generally able to secure loans at very favourable terms, and banks were willing to lend freely under the assumption that bad loans would be covered by superpowers unwilling to see regimes fall to a competing ideology. When the Cold War ended, the insecurity of these assumptions was revealed, and when bailouts were no longer forthcoming, debt crises struck developing nations hard. The World Bank and the IMF suddenly achieved a new relevance as they worked to negotiate debts no longer mediated by interested superpowers.

The terms demanded by the IMF and the World Bank for the renegotiations of loans were based firmly on free trade principles. These terms, which have been called structural adjustments, austerity measures, and conditionalities, have sparked spirited and sometimes violent debate. Nations, particularly the heavily indebted nations of Africa, Central and South America, and Eastern Europe, in order to secure solvency loans, have been required to enact a host of free trade measures, including the devaluation of their currencies, removal of protective tariffs, reductions in public spending, and the privatization of key industries and services, including health care and education.

Those who dispute the effectiveness of these free trade conditions imposed on poorer countries argue that the "conditionalities" have never been fully practiced by the wealthy nations whose representatives dominate the IMF and World Bank. They point out that at no time during the critical years when the United States or Britain were developing their economies were their currencies devalued or key social support programmes privatized. These critics can also point to the vivid and devastating consequences of reductions in public spending, particularly in the area of health care in Africa. For their part, the supporters of free trade doctrines can point to the indisputable economic growth of such major nations as India and China. In the early years of the twenty-first century, it was reliably estimated that one million people a month were being pulled out of poverty by China's embrace of the free market.

REEMERGENCE OF FREE TRADE

Though the neoliberal globalization of the free market

increased rapidly after the fall of the Soviet Union and the opening of China to trade, the intellectual roots for the reemergence of free trade were established decades earlier in Europe and the United States. Important figures include the Austrian economist Friedrich von Hayek, who argued, in works such as *The Road to Serfdom* (1944) that any centralized control over social and economic matters would inevitably lead to totalitarianism. Even more influential was the University of Chicago economist Milton Friedman. Friedman was largely responsible for the shift in academic economics away from Keynesian ideas and towards monetarism, or the idea that money supply rather then employment should be the focus of economic policies. While Friedman's monetarist theories[7] have proved of dubious value, his attacks on virtually all forms of government regulation or even involvement in social and economic life have been very influential indeed. Throughout the years of the Margaret Thatcher and Ronald Reagan administrations in the 1980s, the deregulations advocated by Friedman and his followers were aggressively implemented, and they established the political basis for the free market orthodoxy that dominates national and international economic affairs even to this day.

In the first decade of the twenty-first century, the principles of free market globalization almost exclusively govern the economic practices of nations and the institutions that administer the world's economy, most notably the IMF, the World Bank, and the WTO. However, there are movements of national exception in countries such as Venezuela and Bolivia and activist assertions of dissent such as that expressed in the 1999 WTO protests in Seattle. A strong body of evidence now exists that the current free market orthodoxy has been implemented in ways that violate its core principles of economic freedom. This is especially evident in the removal of barriers to capital flows on the one hand, but the increasing restrictions on the movement of labour on the other hand. Thus, the North American Free Trade Agreement (NAFTA), negotiated among Mexico, Canada, and the United States and implemented in 1994, greatly increased the ability of goods and capital to move across borders even as the increasing militarization of the U.S.-Mexico border has made it more difficult for workers to pursue preferred employments. It remains to be seen if the current expansion of free trade ideas and practices will help or hinder the aspiration for the greatest common good that runs as a consistent theme in the writings of the movement's best thinkers.

Many in the developing world have been welcoming to the ideas of globalization, but are wary of the realities as well. For example, on November 16, 2000, during a lecture at the British Museum, Nelson Mandela said, "We welcome the process of globalisation. It is inescapable and irreversible...." However, he added, "...if globalisation is to create real peace and stability across the world, it must be a process benefiting all. It must not allow the most economically and politically powerful countries to dominate and submerge the countries of the weaker and peripheral regions. It should not be allowed to drain the wealth of smaller countries towards the larger ones, or to increase inequality between richer and poorer regions." These types of concerns have given rise to many criticisms of the current form of globalization, and given a bad name to "free trade" and "free market capitalism" in various circles.

Opposition to Free Trade

Arguments for protectionism fall into the economic category (trade hurts the economy) or the moral category (the effects of trade might help the economy, but have ill effects in other areas); a general argument against free trade is that it is colonialism or imperialism in disguise. The moral category is wide, including concerns of income inequality, environmental degradation, supporting child labour and sweatshops, race to the bottom, wage slavery, accentuating poverty in poor countries, harming national defence, and forcing cultural change.[8]

It is argued that the way the more powerful countries have been pushing for various policies implies that the globalization process is a continual repeat of mercantilist processes seen throughout history.

> The wealth of the ancient city-states of Venice and Genoa was based on their powerful navies, and treaties with other great powers to control trade. This evolved into nations designing their trade policies to intercept the wealth of others (mercantilism). Occasionally one powerful country would overwhelm another through interception of its wealth though a trade war, covert war, or hot war; but the weaker, less developed countries usually lose in these exchanges. It is the military power of the more developed countries that permits them to dictate the terms of trade and maintain unequal relationships.[9]

In that context, the Cold War, for example, can be seen as battles over differences in how resources were going to be used to develop a country; most colonies that broke free around and after First and Second World Wars were often trying to simply develop their nations. Because the imperial powers were to lose out, they would often cry "communism" and use that as justifications for military action or trade embargoes, overthrowing potential democratic regimes in favour of more "stable" dictatorships, and other malleable regimes.

Adam Smith, in his 1776 classic, *The Wealth of Nations*, was highly critical of mercantilist practices of the wealthy nations:

> Though the encouragement of exportation and the discouragement of importation are the two great engines by which the mercantile system proposes to

> enrich every country, yet with regard to some particular commodities it seems to follow an opposite plan: to discourage exportation and to encourage importation. Its ultimate object, however, it pretends, is always the same, to enrich the country by the advantageous balance of trade. It discourages the exportation of the materials of manufacture, and of the instruments of trade, in order to give our own workmen an advantage, and to enable them to undersell those of other nations in all foreign markets; and by restraining, in this manner, the exportation of a few commodities of no great price, it proposes to occasion a much greater and more valuable exportation of others. It encourages the importation of the materials of manufacture in order that our own people may be enabled to work them up more cheaply, and thereby prevent a greater and more valuable importation of the manufactured commodities.[10]

Policies such as structural adjustment, certain types of rules and processes of the WTO etc., are also mercantilist. We are constantly told that we live in a world of global free trade capitalism, and yet we see that while free markets are preached (in Adam Smith's name), mercantilism still appears to be practiced.

Free trade is often opposed by domestic industries that would have their profits and market share reduced by lower prices for imported goods.[11] For example, if United States tariffs on imported sugar were reduced, U.S. sugar producers would receive lower prices and profits, while U.S. sugar consumers would spend less for the same amount of sugar because of those same lower prices. The economic theory of David Ricardo holds that consumers would necessarily gain more than producers would lose.[12] Since each of those few domestic sugar producers would lose a lot while each of a great number of consumers would gain only a little, domestic producers are more likely to mobilize against the lifting of tariffs.[13] More generally, producers often favour domestic subsidies and tariffs on imports in their home countries, while objecting to subsidies and tariffs in their export markets.

Free trade agreements are also often opposed by domestic labour markets in which wages and employment tend to suffer from foreign competition. This holds particularly true for unskilled and trade workers who face the most rivalry from free trade agreements with developing countries. For such instances, those workers face declining employment opportunities and ultimately move to lower wage services industries that are immune to export, such as retail. As a result of labour market saturation, wages decline in the low wage services sector, which reduces the ability for those workers to contribute as consumers. Further, the saturated low wage labour market drives labourers into higher wage construction and services causing an overall decline in real wages throughout. It is theorized by economist Ravi Batra that the overall decline in real wages across all sectors after the 1970s energy crisis was caused by an unprecedented increase in global free trade.[14]

"Free trade" is opposed by many anti-globalization groups, based on their assertion that free trade agreements generally do not increase the economic freedom of the poor or the working class, and frequently make them poorer. Where the foreign supplier allows *de facto* exploitation of labour, domestic free-labour is unfairly forced to compete with the foreign exploited labour, and thus the domestic "working class would gradually be forced down to the level of helotry."[15] To this extent, free trade is seen as nothing more than an end-run around laws that protect individual liberty, such as the Thirteenth Amendment to the United States Constitution (outlawing slavery and indentured servitude). In this regard, protective trade policies are seen, not so much as protecting domestic producers, but rather, as protecting liberty itself. This argument actually comports with the economic analysis of Free Trade to the extent that "slavery and perfect competition equilibria are Pareto optimal."[16] Thus, while admitting that some gain in efficiency might be realized in the short term by implementation of free trade policies, the long-term question of the cost of that efficiency in terms of loss of liberty remains.

It is important to distinguish between arguments against free trade theory, and *free trade agreements* as applied. Some opponents of NAFTA see the agreement as being materially harmful to the common people, but some of the arguments are actually against the particulars of government-managed trade, rather than against free trade *per se*. For example, it is argued[17] that it would be wrong to let subsidized corn from the U.S. into Mexico freely under NAFTA at prices well below production cost (dumping) because of its ruinous effects to Mexican farmers. Of course, such subsidies violate free trade theory, so this argument is not actually against the principle of free trade, but rather its selective implementation.

Latin America performed poorly since tariff cuts in 1980s and 1990s, compared to protectionist China and Southeast Asia. According to Samuelson, it is wrong to assume a necessary surplus of winnings over losings. David Wessel and Bob Davis try to emphasize that trade barriers should exist to help poor nations build domestic industries and give rich nations time to retrain workers.[18]

Reinforcing Colonialism

It has long been argued that free trade is a form of colonialism or imperialism, a position taken by various proponents of economic nationalism and the school of mercantilism. In the nineteenth century these criticized British calls for free trade as cover for British Empire, notably in the works of American Henry Clay, architect of the American System[19] and by German American economist Friedrich List.[20]

More recently, Ecuadorian President Rafael Correa has denounced the "sophistry of free trade" in an introduction he wrote for a book titled *The Hidden Face of Free Trade Accords*, written in part by Correa's current Energy Minister Alberto Acosta. Citing as his source the book *Kicking Away the Ladder*, written by Ha-Joon Chang, Correa identified the difference between an "American system" opposed to a "British System" of free trade. The latter, he says, was explicitly viewed by the Americans as "part of the British imperialist system." According to Correa, Chang showed that it was Treasury Secretary Alexander Hamilton, and not Friedrich List, who was the first to present a systematic argument defending industrial protectionism.

Conclusion

The emergence of capitalism represents a culture that is in many ways the most successful that has ever been deployed in terms of accommodating large numbers of individuals in relative and absolute comfort and luxury. It has not been as successful, however, in integrating all in equal measure, and its failure here remains on of its major problems. It has solved the problems of feeding large numbers of people (although certainly not all), and it has provided unprecedented advances in health and medicine (but, again, not for all). It has promoted the development of amazingly complex technological instruments and fostered a level of global communication without precedent. It has united people in common pursuits as has no other culture. Yet, it remains to be seen when the balance sheet is tallied whether capitalism represents the epitome of "progress" that some claim.[21]

Capitalism has been successful in nurturing technological innovation, in promoting initiative, and in creating wealth (and increasing poverty). Many economists are agreed that in general capitalism can be a powerful engine for development. But, political interests and specific forms of capitalism can have different results. The monopoly capitalism of the colonial era for example was very destructive. Likewise, there is growing criticism of the current model of corporate-led neoliberalism and its version of globalization and capitalism that has resulted. This criticism comes from many areas including many NGOs, developing nation governments and ordinary citizens.

Notes

1. Robbins, Richard H., *Global Problems and the Culture of Capitalism*, Boston: Pearson, 2011, 5th edition, pp. 11–12.
2. Stiglitz, Joseph, *Globalization and its Discontents*, New York: Penguin Books, 2002.
3. *Ibid.* Also, see for example, John Gray's *False Dawn: The Delusions of Global Capitalism*, New York: The New Press, 1998. Gray was an influential conservative political thinker, influencing Margaret Thatcher and the New Right in Britain. Yet, he has argued that the current form of global capitalism is not a naturally occurring process, but an imposed Anglo-American political project.
4. Smith, Adam. [1776] 2000. *The Wealth of Nations*. New York: Modern Library.
5. *Ibid.*
6. Keynes, John Maynard. [1936] 1997. *The General Theory of Employment, Interest, and Money*. Amherst, New York: Prometheus.
7. Friedman, Milton. [1962] 2002. *Capitalism and Freedom*. Chicago: University of Chicago Press.
8. Boudreaux, Don, *Globalization*, 2007.
9. J.W. Smith, *The World's Wasted Wealth 2,* Institute for Economic Democracy, 1994, p. 120.
10. Adam Smith, *Wealth of Nations*, Book IV, Chapter VIII (Everyman's Library, Sixth Printing, 1991), p. 577.
11. William Baumol and Alan Blinder, *Economics: Principles and Policy*, p. 722.
12. Richard L. Stroup, James D. Gwartney, Russell S. Sobel, *Economics: Private and Public Choice*, p. 46.
13. Brakman, Steven; Harry Garretsen, Charles Van Marrewijk, Arjen Van Witteloostuijn (2006). *Nations and Firms in the Global Economy: An Introduction to International Economics and Business*. Cambridge: Cambridge University Press.
14. Batra, Ravi (1993). *The Myth of Free Trade*. New York: Charles Scribner's Sons Macmillan Publishing Company. pp. 70–78.
15. Marx, Karl, *The Civil War in the United States*, p. 23.

16. Haluk, Serdar, *A Microeconomic Analysis of Slavery in Comparison to Free Labour*, Bilkent University, Ankara, Turkey.
17. Institute for Agricultural and Trade Policy NAFTA Truth and Consequences: Corn.
18. "Job prospects: Pain from free trade spurs second thoughts; Mr. Blinder's shift spotlights warnings of deeper downside", David Wessel and Bob Davis. *Wall Street Journal*, 28 March, 2007, p. A1.
19. "Gentlemen deceive themselves. It is not free trade that they are recommending to our acceptance. It is, in effect, the British colonial system that we are invited to adopt; and, if their policy prevails, it will lead, substantially, to the recolonization of these States, under the commercial dominion of Great Britain.", "In Defence of the American System, Against the British Colonial System." 1832, February 2, 3, and 6, Clay, Henry (1843). *The Life and Speeches of Henry Clay*. II. pp. 23-24.

20 "Had the English left everything to itself—'Laissez faire, laissez aller', as the popular economical school recommends—the [German] merchants of the Steelyard would be still carrying on their trade in London, the Belgians would be still manufacturing cloth for the English, England would have still continued to be the sheep-farm of the Hansards, just as Portugal became the vineyard of England, and has remained so till our days, owing to the stratagem of a cunning diplomatist."

21. Robbins, 2011, *Op. cit.*, pp. 11–12.

2

Proposed Free Trade Agreement Between India and the European Union

Economic ties between India and Europe dates back to an early time. The arrival of Portuguese, Dutch, French and English East India Companies changed the nature of trade between India and Europe. This market-determined economic relationship between India and Europe changed with the advent of British colonialism in the subcontinent.[1] At the time of Independence in 1947, a major portion of India's trade was either with Britain or its colonies and allies. This pattern continued for some years. After Independence, Indian leadership adopted a policy of 'self-reliance'.[2] As Independent India established its relations with other countries, trade was diversified. In later years, the former Socialist Bloc countries also became major trading partners. During the Cold War period, India adopted a policy of non-alignment and maintained a close relationship with the former Soviet Union. As a result, its interactions with Europe became limited. Still, trade and economic relations with Europe have always been very important for India and formed the core of India-European Economic Community (EEC)/EU relations.

Realizing the importance of economic relations with European countries, India was amongst the first few countries to establish diplomatic relations with the EEC in 1962. Later, India and the EEC signed some agreements in 1973 and 1981. The Commercial Cooperation Agreement (CCA) of December 1973 (which came into force in April 1974) was the first one to be signed by the EEC with any "non-associated developing country embodying the concepts of commercial and economic cooperation linked with trade."[3] Remarkably, this agreement focused on trade promotion with India in such a way that it would not affect India's bilateral relations with individual EEC member-states. As a comprehensive agreement, "it covered a wide range of economic issues including trade, economic cooperation, industry, services, energy, telecommunication, tourism, private sector investment, science and technology, intellectual property, agriculture, development cooperation, environment and human resource development." It provided for a Joint Commission and three Sub-commissions on the following areas:

(i) Trade and commercial cooperation,
(ii) Economic cooperation, and
(iii) Development cooperation.

Later, six working groups in areas of agriculture and marine products, information technology, environment, textiles and consular issues were also set-up. In 2001, India and the European Union (EU) signed a science and technology agreement. They also signed a Customs Cooperation Agreement in 2004 to simplify customs procedures to facilitate trade as per international standards.

INDIA'S INTEGRATION WITH THE GLOBAL ECONOMY AND TRADE RELATIONSHIP WITH EU

Since the early 1990s, India has embarked on a process of economic reform and progressive integration with the global economy that aims to put it on a path of rapid and sustained growth. Per capita incomes more than doubled during the period 1990-2005. Table 2.1 shows, EU-India trade, which has grown subatantially. An year on year trade from 2007 to 2010 has grown at a CAGR of about 9 per cent. At the €same time according to EUROSTAT, 2012, EU investment to India has more than tripled since 2003 from € 759 million to € 3 billion in 2010 and trade in commercial services has tripled from € 5.2 billion in 2002 to € 17.9 billion in 2010.

Table 2.1: European Union, Trade with India

(in € million)

Period	*Imports*	*Variation*	*Share of total EU Imports*	*Exports*	*Variation*	*Share of total EU Exports*	*Balance*	*Trade*
		(%, y-o-y)	*(%)*		*(%, y-o-y)*	*(%)*		
2007	26587	17.6	1.9	29177	19.6	2.4	2591	55764
2008	29530	11.1	1.9	31263	7.1	2.4	1732	60793
2009	25442	−13.8	2.1	27427	−12.3	2.5	1985	52869
2010	33228	30.6	2.2	34797	26.9	2.6	1569	68025

Source: EUROSTAT, 2012.

Table 2.2 shows India's trade with European Union. As the table shows, India's export to EU has substantially increased over the years, although there is fluctuation as far as import is concerned. This is on account of the financial

Table 2.2: India, Trade with European Union

(in € million)

Period	*Imports*	*Variation*	*EU Share of total Imports*	*Exports*	*Variation*	*EU Share of total Exports*	*Balance*	*Trade*
		(%, y-o-y)	*(%)*		*(%, y-o-y)*	*(%)*		
2007	32428	20.8	18.0	24186	16.9	22.0	−8242	56614
2008	27743	−14.4	14.6	25748	6.5	21.6	−1996	53491
2009	26434	−4.7	14.5	25045	−2.7	21.3	−1389	51479
2010	32071	21.3	12.2	31343	25.1	18.8	−728	63413

Source: EUROSTAT, 2012.

instability in EU. Exports from India have grown at a CAGR of about 9 per cent. And overall trade has grown at a CAGR of about 4 per cent. This is low as compared to EU's overall trade with India as shown in Table 2.1.

Table 2.3 shows a comparative picture of European Union trade with India as compared to other countries in 2011 alone, with a break-up of the trade items.

To addition to trade, in order to assist India in continuing its efforts to better integrate into the world economy with a view to further enhancing bilateral trade and investment ties, the EU is providing trade related technical assistance to India. €13.4 million were allocated through the Trade and Investment Development Programme (TIDP) funded from the Country Strategy Paper (CSP) 2002-2006. At present, the follow-up programme to the TIDP is being designed and will be funded by the Country Strategy Paper 2007-2013.

COOPERATION FRAMEWORK WITH INDIA

In 2004 India became one of the EU's "strategic partners." Since 2005, the EU-India Joint Action Plan, revised in 2008, aims at realising the full potential of this partnership in key areas of interest to India and the EU.

The EU and India have in place an institutional framework, cascading down from the annual EU-India Summit, to a senior-official level Joint Committee, to the Sub-Commission on Trade and to working groups on technical issues such as Technical Barriers to Trade (TBT), Sanitary and Phytosanitary Measures (SPS), agricultural policy or industrial policy. These are the fora where a number of day-to-day issues, such as EU market access problems, are discussed.

In the first summit meeting held in Lisbon in June 2000, India and the EU agreed to enhance their trade and cooperation. As a result, the Eleventh EU Joint Commission encouraged industry to launch the 'Joint Initiative to Enhance "Trade and Investment"'. These meetings led to 'India-EU Strategic Partnership' in 2005. At the Sixth Summit in 2005,

Table 2.3: European Union Trade with India

European Union, Exports to the World: 2011			*European Union, Exports to India: 2011*			
Sections	*Value (millions of euro)*	*Share of Total (%)*	*Sections*	*Value (millions of euro)*	*Share of Total (%)*	*Share of total EU Exports*
TOTAL	1531122	100.0%	TOTAL	40419	100.0%	2.6%
Machinery and transport equipment	647511	42.3%	Machinery and transport equipment	15729	38.9%	2.4%
Chemicals and related prod, n.e.s.	253037	16.5%	Manufactured goods classified chiefly by material	13480	33.3%	6.9%
Manufactured goods classified chiefly by material	195760	12.8%	Chemicals and related prod, n.e.s.	4245	10.5%	1.7%
Miscellaneous manufactured articles	157631	10.3%	Miscellaneous manufactured articles	2665	6.6%	1.7%
Mineral fuels, lubricants and related materials	98650	6.4%	Crude materials, inedible, except fuels	2415	6.0%	5.9%
Food and live animals	63726	4.2%	Mineral fuels, lubricants and related materials	307	0.8%	0.3%
Commodities and transactions n.c.e.	43679	2.9%	Commodities and transactions n.c.e.	296	0.7%	0.7%
Crude materials, inedible, except fuels	40920	2.7%	Food and live animals	234	0.6%	0.4%
Beverages and tobacco	25107	1.6%	Beverages and tobacco	87	0.2%	0.3%
Animal and vegetable oils, fats and waxes	3874	0.3%	Animal and vegetable oils, fats and waxes	22	0.1%	0.6%

* The sums of the individual SITC product categories are less than the totals due to confidentiality reasons.

Source: EUROSTAT (Comext, Statistical regime 4); World excluding Intra-EU trade and European Union: 27 members.

a 'Joint Action Plan' was also launched. "These meetings have been supplemented by 'India-EU Business Summits' organized by apex Chambers of Commerce and Industries on the Indian side and the Union of Industrial and Employers' Confederation of Europe" (UNICE) and local chambers of commerce from the member states representing the Presidency on the EU side.

The 2005 EU-India Summit generated a serious political commitment to increase bilateral trade and economic cooperation and to tackle barriers to trade and investment. Within the Joint Action Plan, the Summit launched a High Level Trade Group (HLTG) and mandated it to explore ways and means to deepen and widen the bilateral trade and investment relationship. The HLTG was also tasked with examining the possibility of launching negotiations on a broad-based trade and investment agreement. With its combination of rapid growth and relatively high market protection India was an obvious partner for one of the new generation of EU FTAs launched as part of the Global Europe strategy in 2006.

The parameters for an ambitious FTA were set out in the report of the EU-India High Level Trade Group in October 2006, which was tasked with assessing the viability of an FTA between the EU and India. Other studies have reinforced the economic potential of an FTA between the EU and India.[4] The HLTG met five times in New Delhi or Brussels and engaged in substantive discussions on a wide range of subjects. The broader trade policy context was examined and information was exchanged on the EU's and India's bilateral trade agreements with other parties. In order to facilitate dialogue, the HLTG exchanged non-papers on trade in goods, trade in services, investment, trade facilitation, public procurement, intellectual property rights, competition and dispute settlement.

KEY HIGHLIGHTS OF THE HLTG

The HLTG observes that trade and investment is a cornerstone of the EU and India's multidimensional relationship. As natural allies in a wide range of global issues, this relationship was upgraded in 2004 to a Strategic Partnership, which led to even closer cooperation on a broad range of areas. Both the EU and India are committed at many levels—Governments, businesses and consumers—to open the door to further engagement. This presents a unique opportunity to bolster trade and investment relations.

Other observations are given below:

- The EU and India, both global players in world trade, have a shared belief in the benefits of the rule-based multilateral trading system and are deeply committed to supporting fair and balanced trade rules for all. Both parties are committed to the successful outcome of the Doha Development Agenda (DDA) negotiations and are convinced that deepening bilateral trade relations should support, rather than undermine, the multilateral route.
- The EU and India constitute strategically important markets for each other's economic operators both in terms of immediate opportunities as well as future potential. Whilst keen to open the door to these opportunities, the EU and India are aware of the need to ensure the benefits are distributed fairly. Both are conscious of the need for growth to respect the environment and be sustainable for future generations.
- India represents the only large and growing emerging economy in Asia where the EU remains the leader both in external trade and foreign investment flows. European businesses cannot afford to ignore the opportunities in one of the most dynamic markets in the world with a growth rate second only to China's. India's great advantages in the market place are that it has a large pool of educated and skilled, English-speaking workers. This has provided a launch pad for service specialisation and also contributed to the growing consumer market. There are, therefore,

opportunities for European firms in terms of investment, including collaboration with Indian partners whether through outsourcing or joint ventures, trade in intermediary products as well as access to a market for consumer goods.

- Looking to the future, there are many intrinsic advantages that will continue to drive India's competitiveness in global trade. A first example can be found in sheer demographics. India has one of the youngest populations in working age (more than 50% of the population under 25) and this situation is predicted to continue. This will provide the Indian economy with a ready supply of competitive labour for years to come. Secondly, India's role at the cutting edge of innovation and research provides a technological edge for many industries. India's imminent transition from being a major business process outsourcing destination to a knowledge process outsourcing destination is part of this trend.
- For India, the EU represents the largest market in the world with a GDP of €10,800 billion in 2005, home to nearly half a billion consumers, with a high average level of income (GDP per capita of €23,377). It constitutes a single market where internal borders have been abolished between 25 countries allowing goods, services, people and capital to move freely, which has helped to make it the largest global destination for foreign investment. The enlargement of the EU and the introduction of the Euro have further improved the climate for trade and investment. Europe's economy combines a strong industrial base with a knowledge-based economy founded on a skilled workforce and a high level of investment in research and development. Internationally, the EU's strengths lie in creativity, innovation and quality.
- The EU considers that open markets are a powerful

stimulus to competition, innovation and productivity growth. In fact, the EU is one of the most open markets in the world, including for Indian exporters.

- EU and India complement each other in their diversified economic structures in terms of output, capital stock, human resources and trade in goods and services. Taking bilateral trade patterns as an example, the EU's exports of goods to India are predominantly intermediary products for further manufacturing whilst India's exports to the EU are in both primary products and finished consumer goods.
- In bilateral services trade, the main products exchanged in both directions were transport services, travel services and business services. In addition, India has shown high growth in information technology, medical services, tourism and some financial services whereas the EU is a leader in professional services such as accounting and legal services, financial services, postal and courier services and telecommunication services.
- In some areas, there is clearly reciprocal trade within the same product and service categories. This can be explained, in some cases, by the structure of the industrial chain; for example, European traders export diamonds to India where they are processed and sent back as finished products. There are other cases when the data does not capture differentiation between products or services, where there is a complementarity in market demand in terms of quality or price.
- The EU and India remain important investment partners with investment flows becoming ever more balanced. EU is India's largest source of Foreign Direct Investment (FDI).
- Whilst this expansion in trade and investment is significant, there are reasons to believe that current levels are below potential: trade is growing rapidly

but remains modest in relative terms. Despite the fact that nearly 1 out of every 6 people on the planet is Indian, India currently punches below its weight in terms of share in world trade. But this is set to change. There are opportunities for enhancing trade and investment in both directions.

POSSIBLE BROAD-BASED TRADE AND INVESTMENT AGREEMENT PROPOSED BY THE HLTG

In the background of the optimistic observations laid down by the HLTG, it discussed a number of specific areas that would be relevant to any future bilateral trade and investment agreement. The thrust of these discussions along with any relevant conclusions are set out by area below.

Trade in Goods

The HLTG proposed for a reduction of trade barriers to bring progressive improvements in trading conditions with the objective of promoting growth, employment and sustainable development. HLTG opined, "Bilateral Free Trade Agreements (FTA) aim to eliminate tariffs between the parties on substantially all trade and thus provide opportunities for current and potential exporters to develop their business and diversify the export Base." The HLTG discussed the principles behind any possible future FTA between EU and India and concluded that any bilateral agreement should be WTO compatible and build upon the outcome of the DDA negotiations. It was further determined that—

- The ambition is to achieve elimination of duties on 90 per cent of tariff lines and trade volume within seven years of the entry into force of the agreement.
- Modalities for the treatment of sensitive products would be agreed including review clauses and partial liberalisation.

The HLTG concluded that there was potential interest in elimination of duties in bilateral trade in light of the complementarity of EU and Indian economies.

Trade in Services

The HLTG analysed the importance of the service sector to both the EU and India and considered the scope for negotiations of a FTA in services. There was unanimity on the principle that any such agreement should build upon the outcome of the DDA, to which both partners are fully committed, and that any agreement should be compatible with GATS. In concrete terms, the parties concurred that any agreement should:

- Ensure substantial sectoral coverage measured in terms of number of sectors, volume of trade and modes of supply. No mode of supply should be excluded; and
- Provide for the elimination of substantially all discrimination between the parties.

Furthermore, the HLTG determined the importance of a common understanding being reached on various points. In particular, the following areas can be the focus for further discussions:

- The use of the current level of opening as the point of departure for additional services commitments.
- Liberalisation commitments in modes 1, 2, 3 and 4 as well as exploring areas of mutual interest to facilitate the mutual recognition of professional qualifications in various sectors and related issues.

The HLTG concluded that there was a potential interest in an ambitious free trade agreement. Nonetheless, both parties recognised the sensitivities of certain service sectors. The HLTG agreed on the importance of the transparency of regulatory requirements which have an impact on trade in services.

Investment

The HLTG recognised the need to promote long-term productive investment that generates stable employment and sustainable growth. Whilst bilateral investment flows already represent a notable share of both parties' total FDI, the HLTG assessed that there were significant opportunities for increasing bilateral investment and that there was clear mutual interest in facilitating these flows further. Thus, the HLTG considered that a chapter on investment should be included in any future agreement. The parties developed certain principles of such a chapter and were of the opinion that it should:

- Improve market access and provide for national treatment to investors;
- Ensure that host and home states retain their right to regulate;
- Foster transparency by clarifying the regulatory framework;
- Aim at freeing the flow of payments and investment-related capital movements; and
- Seek to facilitate the movement of investment-related natural persons.

The HLTG noted India's interest in including provisions on investment protection and promotion in any possible future bilateral trade and investment agreement. The EU is ready to further consider this issue on the understanding that any such provision would have to be complementary to bilateral investment treaties between India and EU Member States.

Trade Facilitation

Trade facilitation promotes transparency, cuts red tape and

simplifies trade procedures, saving both time and money for business. Moreover, procedural barriers in export markets can be a particular burden for SMEs. In addition, trade facilitation measures can reinforce security and promote higher customs revenues and a better investment climate. Cooperation in this area, therefore, has considerable potential to improve supply chains and trade logistics between the EU and India, thereby enhancing trade flows.

Negotiations in the DDA on trade facilitation have been making good progress. The EU and India have been cooperating closely with a view to achieving an ambitious outcome in line with the negotiating modalities. The HLTG agreed that the parties should support and build on this constructive collaboration.

Consequently, the HLTG advocated that the EU and India develop provisions on trade facilitation within any possible future bilateral trade agreement, as a complement to a future DDA Agreement. They should also complement the activities foreseen in the EU-India Customs Cooperation and Mutual Assistance Agreement. Discussions could cover reinforced co-operation with the aim of developing a joint working programme and initiatives in the customs field, the modernisation of customs, simplified procedures, supply chain security, automation, the role of customs in enforcing IPR, and other modern challenges in customs work.

Furthermore, the HLTG observed that trade facilitation must also be based on further inputs from business and other stakeholders to help ensure that it effectively makes trading easier.

Public Procurement

The HLTG examined the role of public procurement policies in ensuring that public money is spent in a transparent, efficient and equitable manner. An open and competitive tendering framework allows public authorities not only to make significant cost savings, but to tap into the full financial and technical potential of the private sector. Companies also benefit from an open procurement regime in that it grants them unhampered access to larger markets and provides a level playing field for economic operators. Finally, a competitive procurement regime facilitates the transfer of state of the art technologies and management practices, thus contributing towards the competitiveness of the knowledge and skills economy.

The HLTG examined how to capture these benefits in the bilateral trade arena noting, in particular, the possibilities for improving reciprocal market access. It agreed that a pragmatic approach should be followed for addressing government procurement. This approach shall *inter alia* include better understanding of each party's procurement practices, examine measures to enhance transparency, as well as examine ways to possible improvements in market access opportunities.

Technical Regulations—TBT and SPS

Cooperation on technical barriers to trade (TBT) and sanitary and phyto-sanitary measures (SPS) aims to prevent and eliminate barriers to trade, while respecting legitimate objectives in terms of protecting health, food safety, the environment etc. As signatories to the WTO-TBT Agreement and SPS Agreements, the EU and India are committed to follow common and accepted principles under the SPS and TBT Agreements.

Recognising the importance of technical cooperation, the HLTG agreed that a chapter on these topics should be included in any possible future bilateral trade agreement with a view to increase bilateral trade.

On TBT-related issues, the HLTG decided that a forum should be set-up for examining current barriers to trade and for exchanging information in general as well as on statutory notifications. The HLTG also agreed on the importance of ensuring that technical regulations not be more trade restrictive than necessary, and recommended a further exploration on how mutual recognition could be established for technical regulations and conformity assessment, including exploring ways to establish suppliers' declaration of conformity, with a view to increasing bilateral trade.

On SPS issues, the HLTG noted that there is a need to enhance bilateral cooperation in order to promote mutual understanding and trust between India and the EU. Both sides would efficiently search for mutually acceptable solutions with a view to facilitating trade. Both sides would exchange information on good regulatory practices, development of specific provisions for application of regionalisation, and for assessment of equivalence.

Intellectual Property and Geographical Indications (GIs)

Ensuring an adequate level of protection of intellectual property plays an important role in developing the right climate for trade and foreign direct investment. Both the EU and India consider that robust intellectual property laws play a decisive role in an economic policy that supports innovation and creativity.

The HLTG agreed that the WTO Agreement on Trade-Related aspects of Intellectual Property Rights (TRIPS) sets minimum standards of protection for each category of right. WTO Members have the right to go beyond these standards if they consider it necessary and appropriate in order to incite innovation, to spur investment and to reward creators and innovators for their work

The HLTG agreed to include provisions on intellectual property in any possible future bilateral trade agreement in a manner that was complementary to the appropriate WTO provisions and respecting national sovereignty. The intention is to move towards the effective protection and enforcement of intellectual property rights. The HLTG also recognised that Geographical Indications (GIs) constituted a potentially important part in bilateral trade and should be covered in any possible bilateral agreement. Both the EU and India are committed to the reinforcement of GI protection as part of the DDA negotiations. Bilaterally, the protection of GIs on each others' markets would be enhanced by the negotiation of an agreement on GIs.

Competition Policy

Competition rules are important to promote growth and efficiency of economies and, in a trade policy context, to ensure that the benefits of liberalisation and related regulatory reforms are not undermined by anti-competitive conduct of private parties. Competition rules are not about increasing market access *per se* but about ensuring the conditions which will enable that access is translated into real, not just theoretical, business opportunities. Robust competition policy also improves the attractiveness for foreign investors by creating transparent and non-discriminatory legal frameworks for foreign operators. Effective domestic competition law regimes are thus, essential to guarantee that commonly defined and agreed forms of anti-competitive behaviour detected in bilateral trade can be addressed, whilst fully respecting national sovereignty. Enhanced cooperation among competition authorities can play a vital part in this direction.

The HLTG agreed that it is fundamental to have comprehensive domestic competition laws, which effectively address anti-competitive behaviour and are based on principles of transparency, due process and non-discrimination on the basis of nationality. Both parties considered that there would be an interest in developing their cooperation in the field of competition under the framework of a possible future bilateral trade agreement. Examples of cooperation provisions include the possibility for competition authorities to exchange non-confidential information and the coordination of enforcement activities.

Dispute Settlement

In accordance with the overall objectives of increasing trade and investment and providing greater commercial and legal certainty, bilateral dispute settlement mechanisms are designed to settle any trade irritant or manage it so as to avoid a spill over on the broader relationship. Consultations or other cooperative means remain the preferred means of resolution but where this is not possible, a dispute settlement mechanism can help enforce the rules.

The HLTG agreed that any possible future bilateral trade agreement should include a binding State-to-State dispute settlement mechanism. It noted the degree of convergence between the parties' approaches to this issue in existing bilateral trade agreements. The details of the architecture of such a mechanism, including appropriate timeframes, mediation/consultation, selection of panelists and openness of procedures, would need to be negotiated at the appropriate stage.

TRADE NEGOTIATIONS AND ROUNDS OF MEETINGS

Negotiations for such FTA were launched in June 2007. These were undertaken under the broad framework provided by the HLTG report. The last EU-India Summit took place on, 26 June, 2012 at Brussels.

At the Ninth India-EU Summit held in Marseille, France, in September 2008, both the partners agreed to a revised 'Joint Action Plan' extending strategic partnership to new areas aimed at promoting peace and comprehensive security, sustainable development, research and technology and cultural exchanges. The summit also approved a joint work programme on energy, clean development and climate change, a horizontal civil aviation agreement and launch of a European Business and Technology Centre in India. Apart from bilateral India-EU issues, the leaders also discussed regional and global issues, especially the situation in Afghanistan and Myanmar,

Iranian nuclear issue, terrorism, food security, climate change and global financial crisis. On the sidelines of the political summit, *Mouvement des Entreprises de France* (MEDEE) International, a French Business Federation, also hosted an India-EU Business Summit.

The Eleventh Round between India and EU was held during November 8–11, 2010 at Brussels. The next round of meeting was held at Brussels in November 2011. In a Statement on the state of play of the EU-India, FTA Negotiations, EU Trade Spokesman John Clancy stated, "This is a very important deal for the EU and India. There are some important issues outstanding and only an ambitious agreement will bring significant benefits. But the EU and India are working with full steam ahead to find solutions which are acceptable to both sides. Intense negotiations will, therefore, continue over the coming months to effectively solve the remaining core issues between now and the EU-India Summit, which is scheduled for 10 February."[5]

The negotiations on India-EU, FTA have reached at an intense stage as both trading partners are hoping to finalize the agreement at the India-EU Summit on February 10, 2012 in New Delhi. This was expected to be the concluding summit but nothing is known because of the secretive nature of the agreement, however, trade to take off in spite of earlier prediction that it would start by early 2011.

The latest meeting between the two trading partners was in Brussels, on 26 June, 2012. In a "Joint Statement on the Outcome of the EU-India Trade Ministerial",[6] EU Trade Commissioner Karel De Gucht and Indian Commerce Minister Anand Sharma expressed their satisfaction that negotiations towards an ambitious EU-India Free Trade Agreement are making good progress.

Commissioner De Gucht and Minister Sharma agreed to hold another ministerial meeting before the end of the year with a view to concluding the negotiations. To this end, they instructed their negotiating teams to identify possible solutions on all remaining issues in the coming months. A number of inter-sessional meetings will be held and chief negotiators will also meet again in September to take stock of the negotiations.

Both sides are keen to find results which are mutually acceptable so as to achieve an ambitious outcome which would give an important boost to trade between the EU and India. This is particularly important in the current economic climate.

The FTA is to be in the form of Regional Trade Agreement (RTA), meaning to say EU comprises 27 member countries.[7]

At present, the negotiations on the India-EU FTA involve the following thematic areas:

- Trade in goods;
- Trade in services;
- Cross border investments;
- Non-tariff barriers;
- Rules pertaining to intellectual property rights;
- Competition policy;
- Trade facilitation and customs co-operation;
- Government procurement;
- Regulatory transparency; and
- Dispute settlement.

For EU, FTAs will help in economic expansion. EU economies are moving away from industrial production to knowledge-based and service sectors. On account of the ongoing financial recession in Europe, there is a political pressure within EU to conclude the FTA. And four EU countries such as United Kingdom, France, Germany and Italy are actively pushing forward for the conclusion of the agreement.

Potential sectors where EU wants to make inroad in India include the following:

- Trade in goods
  - EU's major exports to India include optical, ammunition, musical instruments, chemicals,

pharmaceuticals and plastic, agricultural goods such as wheat and processed food (including whisky), automotive, wood and paper.

- Services—
  - ➢ EU wants complete market access and national treatment for service providers. It wants horizontal access to all services.
- Banking, Finance, Savings and Insurance (BFSI)—
  - ➢ EU wants that European banks and insurance companies should be given national treatment. They should be treated at par with Indian banks.
  - ➢ Trade surplus of majority of the EU countries is from financial and business services.
- Infrastructure (telecommunications and water supply) and extractive industries—
  - ➢ EU is seeking greater access in these sectors.
- Legal services and accountancy—
  - ➢ EU also wants removal of restrictions in these sectors, which are currently closed to foreign nationals.
- Investment: India has already signed bilateral investment agreements with 18 EU member-states—
  - ➢ EU wants market access for European firms to invest in India.
  - ➢ Seeking national treatment and MFN (same rights as India gives to others).
  - ➢ Liberalization of investment regime will have major impacts on NE region.
    - ▪ Investments in three sectors: minerals, water management and retail services.
- Rules pertaining to Intellectual Property Rights (IPR)—
  - ➢ EU demands strong implementation of IPRs regime with WTO plus provisions. It would mean changing Indian laws on IPRs.
  - ➢ EU is seeking IP protection more than 20 years due to cumbersome procedures.

   - EU demands India to strengthen "Data Exclusivity" which means protection of data before product is registered/patented.

At present, EU is the largest trading partner of India and at the same time, the largest investor in India. On the political front, India is ready to enter the FTA since India is vying for a permanent membership at the United Nations Security Council. Other motivating factors include:

- India expects greater exports of goods and services (IT)—
   - India's major exports to EU include textiles and clothing, stones, ceramics and glass, agriculture and food items (rice, soybean, cashew nuts, coffee, tea) etc.
- Indian banks expect to tap the NRI population living in European countries. They want greater market share in workers' remittances.
- Foreign Investment is a two-way street. Indian investments in Europe would benefit. Indian FDI to EU was €9 biliion in 2007. While EU-FDI was €10.9 billion

Big Indian corporate houses (Tatas, UB Group, Mittal, ONGC etc.) are acquiring companies in Europe.

A successful conclusion of the Doha round is believed to have contribute significantly to a more open and stable environment for trade and investment for both the EU and India. India is also a major player in the DDA negotiations and, as a leader of the group of (advanced) developing countries known as the G20, has been one of the "G4", along with the EU, US and Brazil. However, EU feels that India's trade regime and regulatory environment still remain comparatively restrictive. This was viewed in the backdrop of downgrading of Indian rank by World Bank. In 2009 the World Bank downgraded the Indian rank to 165 from 120 in

2008 (out of 183 economies) in terms of the 'ease of doing business'. At the same time EU feels that, tariff barriers to imports, India also imposes a number of non-tariff barriers in the form of quantitative restrictions, import licensing, mandatory testing and certification for a large number of products, as well as complicated and lengthy customs procedures.

Notes

1. Prakash, 1998, quoted in Gulshan Sachdeva, "India EU Economic Linkages: Need to Broaden Strategic Partnership', *International Studies*, Vol. 45, No. 4, 2008, pp. 341-368.
2. Roy, 2002, quoted in Gulshan Sachdeva, "India EU Economic Linkages: Need to Broaden Strategic Partnership", *International Studies*, Vol. 45, No. 4, 2008, pp. 341-368.
3. Some of the perceptions and misperceptions have been 'aptly summarized by India's former Foreign Secretary J.N. Dixit. See Dixit, *Indian Foreign Policies and its Neighbours*, Gyan Books, New Delhi, 2001.
4. Report of the EU-India High Level Trade Group, October 2006.
5. "Statement on the state of play of the EU-India FTA Negotiations." http://trade.ec.europa.eu/doclib/press/index.cfm?id=755&serie=470&langId=en
6. "Joint Statement on the Outcome of the EU-India Trade Ministerial", Brussels, June 26, 2012. http://trade.ec.europa.eu/doclib/press/index.cfm?id=812
7. EU-15 countries are Austria, Belgium, Denmark, Finland, France, Germany, Greece, Ireland, Italy, Luxembourg, the Netherlands, Portugal, Spain, Sweden and the United Kingdom. EU-25 countries are EU-15 plus Cyprus, Czech Republic, Estonia, Hungary, Latvia, Lithuania, Malta, Poland, Slovakia and Slovenia (these ten countries joined EU on 1 January, 2004). EU-27 countries are EU-25 plus Bulgaria and Romania which joined EU on 1 January, 2007.

3

Securitization and Militarization

Trade and Development Experience in Manipur

To discern the potential impact of the India-EU FTA on the North east or Manipur, first of all it is important to have an understanding of the trade and development reality that has operated in the region. For much part, development initiatives have been imposed upon the region in a top-down structure mostly from outside. As a result, underdevelopment marks the economy of the North east region in general and Manipur in particular. Principal reasons cited for underdevelopment of the state in many of the development discourses are that it is land, locked, geographically occupying a formidable mountainous terrain. Apart from the geographical factors, which recent policy initiatives for trade had debunked, for example, the Look East Policy, the situation of "law and order" (in official vocabulary) or insurgency that thrive upon "extortion" and "looting" (in the official vocabulary, again) has been cited as the root cause of underdevelopment in the State. The persistence underdevelopment of the region cannot be meaningfully explained in this simplistic nature or in a very narrow economistic approach but rather through a historically oriented political economy. What has primarily contributed to the underdevelopment is the continuation of colonial legacy in the post-British period and perception on the part of the policy formulators that views the region as of strategic importance, thereby, securitizing and militarizing the development and trade initiatives. Or in other words, underdevelopment has been primarily on account of exogenous factors that do not take into account local needs and aspirations.

Contours of the Economy: Profile of the Economy and Opposing Discourses

The North Eastern Region in general and Manipur in particular lags in development far behind the national average. Manipur is an economically backward state of India. Emerging contours of Manipur's economy depicts a disturbing picture. The state lags behind other states of India in terms of industrialization and infrastructure development. It is predominantly an agrarian society and agriculture being the main occupation of the people of Manipur; it has an important place in the economy of the state. Agriculture sector contributes a major share to the total state domestic product and provides employment to about 52.19 per cent of the total workers in Manipur. But majority are marginal land holders.

The size of the cultivated area is about 7.41 per cent only of the total geographical area of the state. Of this total cultivated area, 52 per cent is confined to the valley. Therefore, half of the total valley area which accommodates 67 per cent of the total population is occupied for agriculture purposes. The pressure on land in the valley is thus quite conspicuous. Of late, agriculture in the state is in a throes of crisis on account of decrease in the size of agricultural land. Population growth, urbanization, acquisition of cultivable land for airfield, school and industrial purposes etc. have inadvertently affected agricultural land in the state. Absence of government policy on land use has made the situation worse.

Following Table 3.1 gives a brief purview of economic health of the state.

Table 3.1: Brief profile of economy of Manipur

Particulars	*Manipur*
Area in sq. km.	22,327
Decennial growth rate of population (1991-2001)	30.02
Population below Poverty Line (%) (2005)	17.2
Literacy Rate (2001) (in percentage)	70.5
Workers (in percentage)	42.18
Road length in km per 100 sq. km.	51.2
Per capita consumption of power in KWH	75
No. of Villages electrified (in percentage)	80.2
Credit Deposit Ratio (in percentage)	39
Per Capita Income (at 2001 prices)	12823
Index of Social and Economic Infrastructure	75.39
Food production (cereals) in Qtls/ Ha	23.3
Fertilizer consumption in Kg/Ha	91.9
Per capita product of Milk in Kg.	29.6
Rice production in Qtls/Ha.	23.2
Banks in Nos.	83
No. of Banks per lakh of population	3.5
Per capita credit in Rupees	680.27

Source: Government of Manipur, Draft Industrial and Investment Policy of Manipur, 2011.

Discourses on development on Manipur or the North east are shaped by people occupying positions of power situated at different centres of power. New Delhi, for example, comfortably views that the region is 'the country's pampered child' and disproportionate amounts of Plan funds have flown into the entire North east, considering that only 10 per cent of the Plan funds are loans while the other states receive 70 per cent as loans. Further, 10 per cent of each Ministry's funds are earmarked for the North east where the population criterion is not applied, so that per capita devolution is far higher for the North eastern states. The opposite view emanating from the region accuses the Centre that the region is underdeveloped and socio-economically backward, and has been virtually isolated from the mainstream of development in the country and as a result denied the opportunity of exploiting its full potential.[1] In addition to these, a third and newer understanding of the region is that insurgency is result of underdevelopment and that the situation of conflict has acted as a firewall against all possible remedies for development.

As far as the developmental status of Manipur is concerned, the existing reality presents a gloomy scenario. *Manipur Development Report* states that economy of Manipur remains largely underdeveloped and agrarian with a weak industrial sector and inflated services sector. The half-hearted attempts at state sponsored industrialization have not been successful in contributing to the economy in any substantive way. On account of the low economic activity, Manipur has a huge developmental and fiscal deficit (Institute for Human Development, 2006, I). This is despite the fact that Manipur is one of the major states in the region, and policy makers in Delhi regard the state as one having considerable strategic importance for India. Growing interest in the state in the past decade or so has been for varied reasons. "The state is rich in bio-diversity and has the resources to produce exportable goods based on horticulture, floriculture and sericulture. It can serve as a transit for 'facilitating' trade and other contacts with the East and Southeast Asian countries with which the region has deep rooted historical and ethnic ties."[2] But such an ardent interest taken in the recent past gives a missive to the people. Many find this new found fascination for the state as informed by the unfolding neo-liberal dictates sweeping over India and as a means of investing her capital in the form of Look East Policy. The Policy does not stand to benefit the people of the North east in general or Manipur in particular.

Many authors have propounded corrective measures so that the state can meaningfully come out of the impasse of underdevelopment. Two diametrically opposing views are prevalent in this regard. One view, such as propounded by Gulshan Sachdeva, emphasises upon the creation of market structures, financial institutions, uniform labour laws, private investment as found in the Himachal Pradesh, opening up of the region, and so on, in the lines of thinking emanating from institutions of Government of India. He recommends that the region will have to focus on integrating itself with the rest of the country and the world. It has to build hard and soft infrastructure and revitalise its agriculture. Above all, North East has to become investor friendly, and stand on its own feet without excessive dependence on the Centre. To link the region with dynamic East Asia, the book has argued for declaring certain areas as free trade areas as well as developing an aggressive strategy for a growth quadrangle involving the North East of India, Myanmar, Southwest China, Northern Thailand and Bangladesh.[3]

The other opposing view keeps the primacy of the State in undertaking development. For example, Priyoranjan Singh opines that policy-makers should meaningfully address the structural dimension of the state as well as put in the right perspectives. He traces the historical and structural distortions suffered by Manipur's economy as how that had led to the emergence of a political economy with vested interest in the perpetration of a tertiarised economy with a weak productive base. During the pre-colonial period, Manipur had a stable food economy with high surplus of agriculture along with an extremely weak and subsistence manufacturing sector. The colonial rule left an economy with a strong agricultural base. However, instead of capitalizing on further strengthening the agricultural sector, the process of tertiarization was intensified thereafter at the cost of a rapidly marginalized productive base. He argues that the productive base of agriculture and manufacture only can be the spring broad of a resurgent economy.[4]

Rationale for the Need for Investment in Manipur

Taking into account the poor availability of basic minimum services and the continuing gaps in infrastructural sectors, which have resulted in industrial backwardness of the Region, in 1996, the Prime Minister of India announced a "New initiative for the North Eastern Region" along with a

Rs. 6100 crore special economic package including Rs. 703 crore for Manipur.

Under the new initiatives, the Central Government appointed a High Level Commission to critically examine the backlog in respect of the basic minimum services and the gaps in important sectors of infrastructure development in the region and suggest policies, programme and the requirement of funds to bridge such gaps and backlogs. The Commission has in its report entitled "Transforming the North east" (March 1997)[5], made an exhaustive 173 recommendations touching upon 27 areas for development. These, among others, include power, roads, civil aviation, railways, waterways, telecommunications, banking and financing, trade and transit, industry etc. The report recommends a total of about Rs. 9,396 crore for the whole region's requirement in respect of basic minimum services, of which Rs. 1,423 crore is for Manipur.[6] It also makes room for an indicative requirement of Rs. 93,619 crore as total estimated investments in infrastructural sectors for the region as a whole, of which Manipur's share is Rs. 5,815 crore.[7] The following sector-wise allocations are included in the Report in respect of Manipur:

(1) Irrigation Sector	: Rs. 566 crore
(2) Flood Control	: Rs. 45 crore
(3) Railways	: Rs. 935 crore
(4) Power Sector	: Rs. 3,740 crore
(5) Transmission Sector	: Rs. 84 crore
(6) Others	: Rs. 445 crore

Further, the High Level Commission has advocated to improve the NH-39, the Imphal-Moreh sector in particular, to serve both as a commercial highway and as line of communication for construction of the Rs. 92 crore Tamu-Kalewa Highway sanctioned by Border Road Development Board, as Moreh could become a major nodal point for trade with the South East Asia along the proposed Trans-Asian

Highway.[8] In the banking and finance sector, the Commission has, *inter alia*, spelt out the need to consider industrial finance as part of priority sector lending. The recommendation on the industry sector recognises the need to establish export processing or special economic zones in the region to attract export oriented industries. The Government of Manipur is also vigorously pursuing to set-up such an Export Processing Zone at Moreh.[9]

The Nehruvian model of development for the North east, which was built on the edifice of non-interference into the traditional socio-economic structure of the Region, underwent changes with India's new economic policy initiatives in the post-1991 era and especially after the High Level Commission's Report to the Prime Minister. The Government of Manipur endorsed the Report and was committed to[10]:

- Create a liberal investment environment for economic activity especially industrial activity;
- Minimise government regulation and control;
- Move towards a supportive role, i.e. facilitation;
- Create internationally competitive basic infrastructure facilities;
- Extend preferential treatment to priority sectors of industrial activity through an incentive mechanism; and
- Provide full freedom of industrial and commercial activity within clearly established and transparent parameter.

Keeping in view these new policy initiatives of the Government of India, the State Government adopted the "Industrial Policy of Manipur, 1996." This policy among others seek to create an integrated investor-friendly environment, bring about industry and trade supportive infrastructural establishments and other facility centres, take positive steps to optimise the advantages offered by the recently opened Indo-Myanmar Border Trade through Moreh in Manipur, provide a comprehensive and attractive package of incentives to the industries and others.[11] A package of incentives was offered by the State Government over and above those provided by the Government of India. As a follow up, the Government of Manipur identified agro and food processing, horticulture and floriculture, border trade, energy sector, handloom sector, handicrafts sector, IT sector, mineral sector and tourism sector as key areas of investment.[12]

Colonial Legacy of Underdevelopment

Manipur's economy from its association with British colonialism has been a long journey of peripheral economy and its economic destiny being dictated by exogenous factor and fails to evolve its own. Manipur during the pre-colonial period has a rich history of self-sufficient, self-regulating, self-sustaining and stable economy leaving aside few critical phases of hostility with neighbouring countries especially Burma (now Myanmar). Its economy during the pre-colonial period was characterized by peasant economy; household manufacturing and trade both internal and external formed the other important aspects of the economic life of people. Strength of the economy was on its productive base and supplemented by exchange. The core of the peasant economy, crop husbandry reached its zenith wayback in the early pre-colonial period with the people mastering the art of irrigation for paddy cultivation.[13] Rice economy formed not only the backbone of the agrarian economy but for the economy as a whole. Export of livestock and forest products form the other important source of income for the region. Though the use of currency was evident in the pre-colonial period, the economy was not monetized thoroughly as a result there was no commoditization and commercialization. Mode of production existed in the pre-colonial period was non-exploitative and progressive in nature and existing institutional set-up of that time complemented the smooth and efficient working of the economy.[14] Notwithstanding its smallness, the economy had the potency for transforming into a structurally well balanced economy in the long run. Economy was self-regulating and external element determining the working of the economy was negligible.

Advent of British colonial rule after 1891 Anglo-Manipuri War brought about major structural changes in the economy subservient to their interest. The thrust of British colonial rule was to penetrate the pre-capitalist formation to organize the condition of surplus extraction and accumulation. This was possible through introduction of private property in land, monetization of economy through commercialization of agriculture and taxation. British colonial rule managed to extract huge surplus from rice export and taxation and the revenue generated were utilized for colonial administration rather than for the welfare of the native people. Monetization of the economy had serious implication breaking the cycle of reproduction existed before colonial economic system. Class distinction emerged with the introduction of outside trading class for smoothening rice export and influx of consumer goods from the British India and Europe. With the breakdown of the internal strength of economy after British rule, its economy was slowly but surely transformed into a dependent economy followed by external forces and agents consolidating its base. Institutions in the pre-colonial period that served as an engine of reproduction cycle was dismantled rather than modernized. British colonial rule reduced Manipur into peripheral economy for the metropolitan capital of British India. Manipur experienced a short stint of independent nation from 1947-49, the agrarian economy of erstwhile pre-colonial period was reviving from the ravage of Second World War.

British colonial rule had left an economy that was structurally distorted, but possessed a strong agricultural base from where a development path could have evolved. In a similar fashion Thingnam Kishan opines that underdevelopment alongside a systematic plundering of the region's (*sic* North east) resources formed the matrix of dependency during British colonial period. Post-British policies failed to transform this dynamics as economic development was reduced to the successful establishment of a market for products manufactured elsewhere. He raises the fundamental issue of production as the basis of meaningful development and argues that unless production assumes centrality, development will remain lopsided. Meaningful utilization of the region's resources by generating production remains the logical way out of the current impasse.[15]

Merger with the Indian Union only worsen the already fragile economy with Indian state continuing the trend of colonial legacy. The newly independent India which claimed to be a modern nation state in the making had not shed away the colonial policy followed to the Manipur but rather appropriated and internalized the colonial policy. Merger with India had implication of a small economy integrating with a big economy of India. Merger with India completely undermined its importance not only in the national arena but also for the local populace. Manipur's economy was completely reduced to a peripheral status through the complete monopoly of its development destiny at the mercy of the Centre as Manipur was a Union Territory. Manipur's economy served as captive market for the newly emerging metropolitan capital of India. More precisely merger with India was an economic tragedy. Centralized planning of the immediate post-merger was a continuation of British legacy which was evident from the sheer neglect of productive base of the economy. Policy followed after merger only derided the aspirations of the people and helped in consolidating external agents and few sections of local elites. Free flow of fund in the region in the post-statehood phase with the inception of NEC and DONER helped only the vested interest group and neglect of productive base continues.

At present, the economy is sustaining on inordinate growth in the tertiary sector propelled by central fund, the contribution of agriculture and industry is diminishing. This trend of central fund backed tertiary growth can collapse anytime. Evolving trend is an outcome of long term neglect of productive base of the economy. Secondly, economic planning regarded as the ultimate tool for economic development has been reduced to end itself not means. Five Year Plan in the State are not meticulously framed is devoid of physical and clear-cut targets and lack of direction. Economic planning has been merely reduced to economic rituals and it has not contributed significantly to economic health of the region. Regional planning under the aegis of NEC has also not contributed to the growth especially the productive base of the economy. Funds are largely invested in infrastructural and administration for appeasing the ruling elites of the region. Thirdly, there is no a concrete policy for strengthening the productive base of the economy, *viz.* agriculture and industry. The state has not a draft agricultural policy which will have a long run impact in pursuing for a self-reliant economy. Development policies for agriculture and industry of the State are *ad hoc*, piecemeal and ceremonial in nature. Strengthening of these two sectors will create a long chain of linkages both backward and forward helping in generating gainful employment and income. The focus has been on infrastructure and government services that too without a long term vision. Infrastructure cannot be neglected but disproportionate attention reflects the interest of commission mongering vested interest ruling elites. And finally, development process of the region is shaping in a top down developmentalism of the Indian State. Its destiny and mapping of the course of economic development is being framed by intellectual hegemony of the mainland India devoid of people's aspiration. The economy of the region has never been made to stand on its own and its potential is being externalized and underutilized.

It is worthwhile to recall that wayback in 1997, a High Level Commission Report submitted to the Prime Minister of India, pointed out that North east cannot be treated merely as a resource region, market dump and transit yard. There is strong resentment over what is seen as an earlier phase of 'colonial exploitation' in which its wealth was extracted for others' enrichment.[16] Thus, initiatives have to be undertaken by the Indian State to shed its cloak of colonial designs of domination and extraction, thereby ushering in era of development for the region.

Securitization of the Development Initiatives

The debate on the merging of security and development policies has been in vogue in academic and policy circles with respect to strategies and techniques for conflict prevention, resolution and post-war reconstruction. Some have cited the nexus between security and development as preventive strategies and have underlined the interdependence of the two in a circular fashion, emphasizing that there is no development without security and no security without development. And, therefore, the main emphasis has been at the human level, where concepts like human security and human development are the focal points of analysis. But, others have argued for an integration of a right based approach, improving governance and a need to co-ordinate various mechanisms, actors and agenda related to developmental and security policies. (Another study, which brought the linkage between security and developmental policies to the fore was a World Bank Study in 2005).[17] It concludes that the assessment of structural violence (invisible violence, which occurs when people are deprived of their basic standard of living due to under-development) and not just physical violence (use of force) is essential for a better understanding of the security concerns of the poor.

Security emerged as the guiding principle for all policy interventions, development or otherwise, in the North east region. In the 1950s the Government of India (GoI) evolved and adopted an approach towards the North east Region (NER) which was founded on two edifices. The first edifice, popularly known as the Nehruvian model, was one of non-interference into the traditional socio-economic structure of the region. The second was national security perspective. After India undertook Structural Adjustment Programme (SAP) in the 1990s, the first edifice underwent an overhaul, especially since 1997. However, the second edifice has remained fundamentally unchanged.

Since the NER could not articulate itself its own development future and given the low level of understanding and appreciation of the region among the policy-makers in Delhi, the surest shortcut to policy was one based on security. So, security emerged as the guiding principle for all policy interventions, development or otherwise, in the region.

The security principle, or rather the insecurity of the GoI, drove it to adopt the Armed Forces (Special) Powers Act (Assam and Manipur) wayback in 1958 when there was hardly any insurgency in the region. The GoI could never get rid of its insecurity and abandon the security principle even when it belatedly realized that the NER needed a development agency for transformation. As a result, when the North Eastern Council (which should have been there in 1958 instead of the Armed Forces Special Powers Act) was established in the early 1970s, it was placed under the Home Ministry. But the Home Ministry could never evolve a development strategy for the region as it is neither competent nor oriented for such a task. This politicisation of economic issues has reached its height recently with the requirement of certificates from the Home Ministry for the provincial government to get funds sanctioned from the Ministry of Finance.[18]

The GoI's approach of basing policies towards the region on security principle has stunted the evolution of a spontaneous economic awareness in the region, has kept the people of the region occupied in tackling the transitory political issues, and has thus kept them away from articulating any kind of economic agenda for mutual cooperation and competition. Under such circumstances, any investment and trade agreement, in this context the India-EU FTA, that impinges upon the state of Manipur, has to take into consideration the issue of human rights given that militarization of high level has taken place in the state on account of the existence of the Armed Forces Special Powers Act, 1958 (to tackle armed opposition movements) as well as the key role played by the Ministry of Home Affairs in terms of financial matters.

Military Deployment in Manipur

Consequent to the imposition of the Armed Forces (Special) Powers Act 1958 (AFSPA) from the 1980s, Manipur has become more akin to an occupied territory by the Indian Armed Forces. Assam Rifles, a para-military force under the Ministry of Home Affairs, has the highest prevalence and includes Inspector General Assam Rifles—South Camps, 57th Mountain Division, 59th Mountain Brigade, 73rd Mountain Brigade, 44th Mountain Brigade, 26 Sector Assam Rifles and 57 Mountain Artillery. They are stationed in every known hill ranges of the State. In addition, there is an independent Operation (Army) at Leimakhong, Special Force—Para Troopers, ten battalions of Central Reserve Police Force under one Inspector General, two Battalions of Border Security Force and Indian Reserve Battalions.[19] The deployment of the security forces are for counter-insurgency operations in Manipur. The State Police personnel are not included in this count. The intensity of militarization in Manipur can be reflected from the two Figs. 3.1 and 3.2.

Human Rights Situation in Manipur

The Human Rights Situation in Manipur is aptly captured by the Joint Stakeholders' Report on "Status of Human Rights in Manipur (North Eastern Region) submitted to the Office of the High Commissioner for Human Rights, 2nd Cycle Universal Periodic Review (UPR), Human Rights Council, United Nations, India on November 28, 2011 by Civil Society

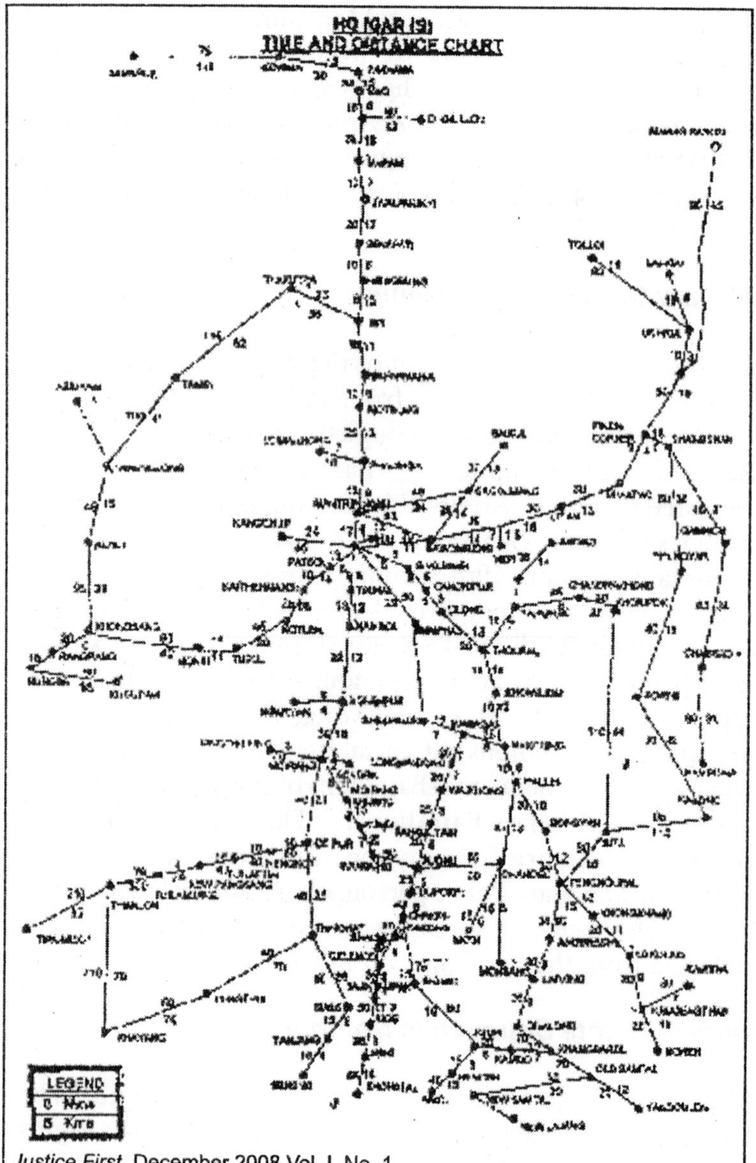

Justice First, December 2008, Vol. I, No. 1

Fig. 3.1: Deployment of Assam Rifles in Manipur

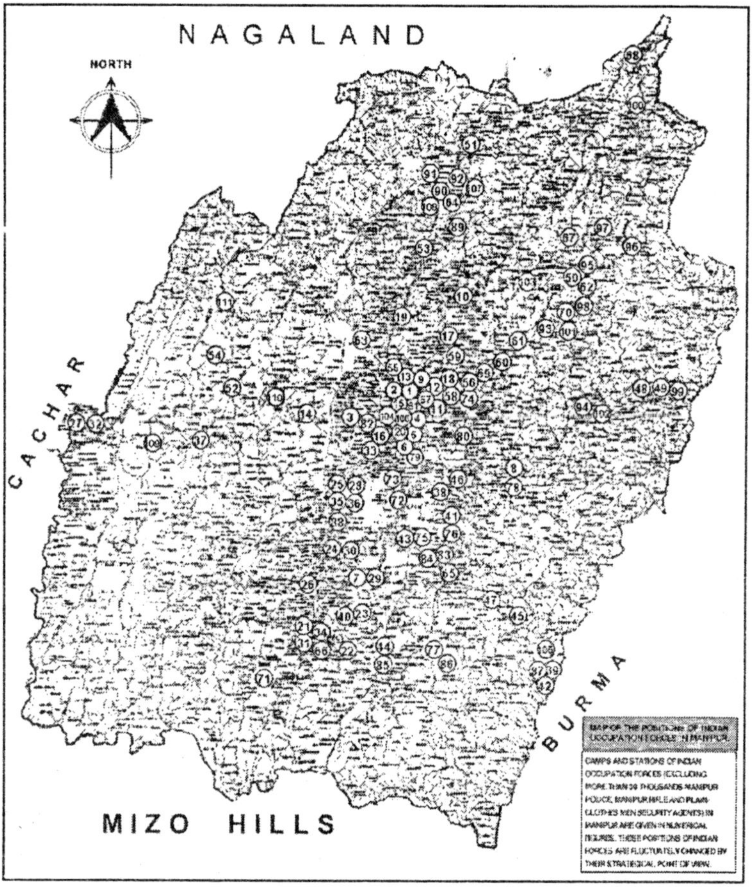

Fig. 3.2: Map showing location of Indian Military Forces in Manipur

Source: Robinson, Andrew (2005), *The Rhizomes of Manipur, Seminar Paper,* Institute of Asia Pacific Studies, University of Nottingham. *www.nottingham.ac.uk/shared/shared_iaps/.../Manipur_illustrated.pdf.*

Note: Each number represents the location of a base or a battalion. Notice the concentration in the centre of the country, suggesting an occupying regime rather than defence of the border.

Coalition on Human Rights and UN. The report observes the following:

1. The promulgation of AFSPA for the last 53 years in Manipur, which grants the Indian Armed Forces special powers to kill on mere suspicion, search without warrant, destroy property institutionalises impunity, blatantly violates the non-derogable rights to life, right against torture, right against arbitrary detention and right to fair trial as provided by the ICCPR.
2. During the first UPR, GOI submitted that the Supreme Court has upheld the constitutionality of AFSPA. However, India has failed to inform the international bodies the recommendations of the officially constituted Committee to Review AFSPA (2005), headed by Justice Jeevan Reddy, which stated that "It is true that the Hon'ble Supreme Court has upheld its constitutional validity but that circumstance is not an endorsement of the desirability or advisability of the Act. When the constitutional validity of an enactment is challenged in a Court, the Court examines (i) whether the Act is within the legislative competence of the Legislature which enacted it and (ii) whether the enactment violates any of the provisions of the Constitution. The Court does not – it is not supposed to—pronounce upon the wisdom or the necessity of such an enactment. It must be remembered that even while upholding its constitutional validity, the Hon'ble Court has found it fit and necessary not merely to approve the "Do's and Don'ts" in the instructions issued by the Army Headquarters from time to time but has also added certain riders of its own, viz. those contained in clauses 8, 9 and 14 to 21 in para 74 of its judgement [at pages 156 and 157 of the judgement in *Naga Peoples' Movement of Human Rights vs. Union of India* (1998) 2 SCC 109]. The Committee is of the

opinion that legislative shape must be given to many of these riders. We must also mention the impression gathered by it during the course of its work, viz. the Act, for whatever reason, has become a symbol of oppression, an object of hate and an instrument of discrimination and highhandedness. It is highly desirable and advisable to repeal this Act altogether..."

3. The view of this Committee has been concurred by other official bodies of India, such as the Second Administrative Reform Commission, 2007 as well as the Prime Minister's Working Group on Confidence Building Measures in Jammu & Kashmir, 2007.
4. AFSPA in Manipur and India's North east region violates Article 4(a) of ICCPR on declaration of "State of Emergency" since *de facto* emergency has been imposed without formal promulgation of any form of public emergency. Under Section 3 of AFSPA, the entire Manipur has been declared as a "disturbed area" since 1980. Section 6 of AFSPA specifies that, "No prosecution, suit or other legal proceeding shall be instituted, except with the previous sanction of the Government, against any person in respect of anything done or purported to be done in exercise of the powers conferred by this Act." This impunity provision is found to be incompatible with the obligations of the Government under Article 2 (3) of the ICCPR to ensure the provision of an effective remedy in cases involving violations of human rights.
5. *Extrajudicial Executions*: In the continuing pattern of extra-judicial executions since the last UPR review till December 2010, the Government of India has extra-judicially executed more than 668 persons.
6. The law enforcing agencies in Manipur are also responsible for a wide range of human rights violations, often committed in close coordination with the Indian Armed Forces. The Manipur police

commandos are also primarily responsible for a series of extra-judicial executions in the pretext of encounter killings in Manipur. The case of the extra-judicial execution of Chungkham Shanjit and Thockchom Rebina on 23 July, 2009 by Manipur police commandoes, in the middle of Imphal in full public view, remains an infamous case and stark evidence of how the law enforcing agencies perpetrate human rights violations with impunity in Manipur.

7. The National Human Rights Commission has written a letter (refer No. 22/14/2004-2005-DBII/FC dated 28 January, 2010) to the Chief Secretary of Manipur asking why the Government of Manipur has not submitted reports of 111 cases of police encounter killings. Inquiries regarding extra-judicial executions are conducted by an Executive Magistrate rather than a Judicial Magistrate, violating Section 176 of the Criminal Procedures Code (Amended in 2005). Executive Magistrates have limited knowledge of law and are not mandated to make judicial opinions. The prevailing climate of impunity coupled with the lack of witness protection discourages witnesses to cooperate in the inquiries. The ignorance of the families on legal matters and imposed time limitation, under the Protection of Human Rights Act, 1992, of making complaints render most extra-judicial executions unregistered. All inquiries completed are never made public, and action taken reports are not placed in the public domain. The former Special Rapporteur on Extra-Judicial Executions, Mr. P. Alston, reported to the UN Human Rights Council in 2007 that despite the Government of Manipur ordering numerous inquiries into alleged extra-judicial executions, none of them ultimately reached any meaningful conclusions.

8. Extra-judicial executions in Manipur, mostly of young men, resulted in the proliferation of young widows and orphans. The widows face the double burden of being a young widow in a traditional patriarchal society as well as the stigma of being branded as families of terrorists. They are denied access to social welfare schemes. The families of the victims of extra-judicial executions formed an association in 2009 called 'Extra-judicial Executions' Victim Families Association, Manipur' (EEVFAM). Their requests to register under the Societies Registration Act, 1989 were denied by the Government of Manipur, thereby also denying their right to freedom of association.
9. *Enforced Disappearances*: Notwithstanding Government of India's commitment to ratify CED, no concrete position steps have been taken by the Government of India to ratify the CED. On the other hand, the phenomenon of enforced disappearances continues in Manipur. The practice of secret detention and elimination persists.
10. The practice of torture continues with impunity. In Manipur, almost every person who is arrested or detained is tortured; and the common methods include verbal abuse, psychological torture, blind-folding, hooding, beating, electric shocks to the genitalia, water-boarding etc. Only a few survivors of torture dare to make formal complaints to the authorities; however, the institutional response of the lower judiciary as well the State and National Human Rights Commissions is to re-traumatise the complainant, discourage and demoralise them.
11. *Human Rights Defenders*: Human Rights defenders are targeted for promoting and defending indigenous peoples' rights. Human Rights defenders are labelled as terrorists, and charged under criminal laws. Human Rights defenders are also arbitrarily arrested, detained

and subjected to severe torture. Human Rights defenders and their organizations are subjected to close monitoring and surveillance including phone and e-mail tapping, e-mail and postal intercepting, hacking, post-restrictions and postal theft, restrictions to movement etc. Right to Information activists have been subjected to systematic targeting by the incorrigibly corrupt and abusive state bureaucracy through threats, arbitrary detention and torture.

12. *Torture and arbitrary detention of Miss Irom Sharmila*: The continued solitary confinement and detention of Miss Irom Sharmila who has been on a hunger strike demanding the repeal of AFSPA since November 2000 constitutes severe mental and physical torture. Miss Sharmila has been charged for attempt to commit suicide under Section 309 of the Indian Penal Code and kept in detention for the past 11 years. An executive order issued by the Home Department, Government of Manipur, dated 8 October, 2004 "not to allow anybody" to meet her without "clear permission of the Home Department" severely curtails her basic human rights and fundamental freedoms including her right to communicate with her family, friends and supporters.
13. The Manipur Human Rights Commission (MHRC) and Manipur State Women's Commission were established, but the MHRC has remained defunct since 2010 as no new member has been appointed by the Government despite an order of the Gauhati High Court. The MHRC also receives most inadequate financial and personnel support from the government, despite repeated appeals by the members of the Commission.
14. The State and National Human Rights Commissions are not in compliance with the Paris Principles. Section 19 of the PHRA 1993 specifically barred the armed

forces of the Union from the jurisdiction of the Commission.

The Indo-Myanmar Border Trade Experience

Securitization of trade initiative is aptly demonstrated by the Indo-Myanmar Border Trade Agreement between the Governments of the Republic of India and Government of Myanmar. The Trade Agreement was signed on January 21, 1994 with the goal of formalization of border trade practices and set such trading activities in a congenial mode. The agreement specified that trade should be conducted through the designated customs posts, viz. (a) Moreh in India (Manipur State) and Tamu in Myanmar, (b) Champhai in India (Mizoram State) and Hri in Myanmar, and (c) other places that may be notified by mutual agreement between the two countries. Following the signing of the agreement the two Land Customs Stations (LCS) at Moreh and Champhai on Indian soil were notified. However, the Champhai station has not become functional till date and all officials or formal Indo-Myanmar Border Trade has been taking place through the Moreh-Tamu route.

The *Draft Industrial and Investment Policy of Manipur, 2011* states that Manipur has the advantage of acting as India's Gateway to the East through Moreh town, which is the only feasible land route for trade between India and Myanmar and other South East Asian Countries. It shares 398 km long international border with Myanmar. A Land Customs Station (LCS) already exists at Moreh for the existing traffic volume of trade.

There are 40 (forty) tradable items under Barter Trade mechanism through Moreh (India-Myanmar Border). Major exportable items include cement, engineering goods, transport equipment, motor cycles, iron and steels, medicines, chemicals and allied products, cotton yarn etc. The major items now imported from Myanmar through barter mechanism are betel nuts, turmeric, red kidney beans (Rajma), kuth roots, gram, resin, dry ginger etc. The volume of trade at Moreh-Tamu

Border Point in 2001-02 was Rs. 95.48 million and in 2009-10 Rs. 298.19 million—an average increase of 39 per cent per annum.[20] Further, Ministry of Finance, Government of India has also cleared the operational of "Normal Trade" through Land Customs Station, Moreh.

India's "Look East" Policy and several new measures taken by both the Central and State Governments to promote and enhance trade link with South East Asia, provide Manipur with a competitive advantage.[21] In recognition of the potential of Moreh, the Government of India has notified an ICP at Moreh.

Trade Agreement was accompanied by simultaneous increase in the number of security personnel at least on the Indian side of the border. The logic behind the increase in the number of security personnel (overt militarization) must be seen in the context of a militarized society like Manipur, where there are demands for self-determination and human rights are violated by the security personnel, who in turn (state forces) receive immunity from the existing Armed Forces (Special) Powers Act.

Regarding the issue of militarization on account of border trade, the Government of India provides the following rationale:

1. To prevent smuggling of arms (by both land and water).
2. To prevent drug trafficking and narco-terrorism.
3. To stop illegal immigration. The Government perceives that there is illegal influx of immigrants into Manipur from Yunnan *via* Northern Myanmar.
4. To protect the Integrated Trade Facility on the India side of the border, which was set-up after acquiring 45 acres of land.
5. And finally, to protect "organised" trade between the two countries.

But the unsaid part of the rationale is to fight insurgency, which involves "collateral damages" (official term to describe loss of civilian lives and destruction of property). Thus, militarization in the name of protecting trade is to curb insurgency in the North Eastern states of India, many of which have established camps in Myanmar and operating from the Myanmarese territory.

As a result, multiple check posts have been erected on the National Highway–39 (NH-39) as well as on National Highway–53 (NH–53). Reports indicate that there are at least 53 check posts of various departments of the Governments of Manipur and Nagaland from Moreh to Dimapur on NH-39 and as many as 12 check-posts of the Government of Manipur on NH-53. These are in addition to the setting up of Integrated Check Post (ICP) at Moreh one of the 12 Integrated Check Posts being developed by Central Government along India's international borders. An Integrated Check Post (ICP) is developed at Moreh. It is one of the 13 Integrated Check Posts being developed by Central Government along India's international borders. These ICPs are being developed by the Ministry of Home Affairs through the Land Ports Authority of India (LPAI). The proposed ICP will facilitate speedy movement of export-import consignments and redress the inconveniences suffered by general public in the emerging scenario of India's Look East Policy. State Government has identified 45.50 acres of land near Gate No. 1 within Customs notified area. Rail India Technical Economic Services (RITES, a Central Public Sector undertaking) have prepared a Detailed Project Report (DPR) for Moreh ICP costing Rs. 136 crore and is under the process of implementation.[22] However, the prevalence of such a large number of check points manned by the security personnel fails to protect delivery of goods to Manipur, when the highways are put under economic blockade from time to time.

Out of many check-posts, manned by the army, Assam Rifles, Manipur Police, Manipur Rifles etc. between Imphal and Moreh, checking are done in the following posts:

- Customs Preventive Force, Moreh;
- Moreh Police Gate, Moreh;

- 24 Assam Rifles, Khudengtabi;
- 165 G-coy, Assam Regiment, Lokchao;
- Tengnoupal Police Station, Tengnoupal;
- 18 Assam Rifles, Tengnoupal;
- 44 Assam Rifles, Bongyang;
- Police out post, Pallel; and
- Pallel customs.

As a corollary, or in order to facilitate further of the trade, Government of Manipur has proposed to set-up a supermarket complex and godowns and an Indian Reserve Battalion Headquarters at Yairolpokpi in Jiribam.

The trade agreement initially provided for cross border trade in 40 products, mostly agricultural/primary commodities produced in the trading countries (not the third country products that dominate the informal border trade). In practice, the agreement actually does not go much beyond according to a formal sanction to exchanges traditionally going on between the local populations in the border areas of the two countries.

Underneath the broader contours of trade, there is a strategic orientation on the part of the Indian State to fight threats which in the official discourse is termed as internal "law and order" problem that plagues whole of the North east India, which have led to overt militarization in the region, especially Manipur as the Champhai station in Mizoram has not become functional till date and all official or formal Indo-Myanmar border trade has been taking place through the Moreh-Tamu route. This becomes evident if one takes into account that major volume of trade between India and Myanmar takes place through the sea route instead of the land route passing through the North east region (*See* Tables 3.2 and 3.3). Trade statistics show that India's exports to the East and Southeast Asia is dominated by mineral fuels and oil, metallic products, jewellry products, chemicals, iron and steel, ships, boats and floating structures, electrical machinery and equipment, vehicle parts, food and animal fodder and cottons products. Tea, coffee and rubber constitute a very small portion of India's exports to East Asia. Majority of India's export items consist of manufacturing goods. It is obvious, therefore, that the North east does not have a comparative advantage in any of India's exports to these countries, given the fact that the share of manufacturing in the domestic product of the region has been growing by a little over one per cent.

As Table 3.2 shows, from year 2005-06 to 2010-11, there has been a negative trend in the Indo-Myanmar Border Trade. From initial promising figures of trade value in 2005-06 and 2006-07 at US$ 15.41 million and US$ 15.77 million, respectively, by 2010-11, the total value of trade stands at a dismal US$ 12.8 million. Between 2005-06 to 2010-11, CAGR of the total value of trade stands at (–) 3.67 per cent.

Table 3.2: Myanmar-India Border Trade

Year	*Export (US$ million)*	*Import (US$ million)*	*Total Trade (US$ million)*
2005-2006	11.28	4.13	15.41
2006-2007	11.02	4.75	15.77
2007-2008	10.91	3.92	14.83
2008-2009	5.49	4.43	9.82
2009-2010	7.79	5.95	13.73
2010-2011	8.03	4.50	12.80

Source: Ministry of Commerce and Industry, Government of India, 2012.

On the other hand, as Table 3.3 shows, in spite of decline in total trade in terms of value in the year 2010-11 at US$ 1058 million, from year 2006-07 to 2010-11, the total trade between the two countries have grown at a CAGR of 3.17 per cent.

In addition to the divergence one finds in the overall trade scenario, another matter of concern is the participation of local traders. Indeed, the locals have thrived in providing

Table 3.3: Myanmar-India Trade by other routes

	Trade by other routes		
Year	*India's Export (US$ million)*	*India's Import (US$ million)*	*Total (US$ million)*
2006-07	128.93	777.18	905.42
2007-08	174.52	806.02	980.54
2008-09	216.15	924.54	1140.79
2009-10	200.18	1283.85	1484.04
2010-11	186.45	871.63	1058.08

Source: Ministry of Commerce and Industry, Government of India, 2012.

secondary and tertiary services in terms of setting up of hotels and other form of kiosks or in supplying logics support to the movement of goods. However, participation in terms of investment and running worthwhile business remains negligible.

North east in general and Manipur in particular is a primarily agrarian based economy with rich bio-diversity. Presence of manufacturing industry is nearly absent. In other words, agriculture remains a priority sector for the region and overall, there is very high dependence on agriculture and allied activities. However, in the list of commodities that has been agreed to be exported from India, none of the local products find a space. Wheat flour, buffalo appall, seeds, sugar, common salt etc. are more in demand in Myanmar.

Moreover, earlier, "Moreh Trade", in its unorganized form, provided livelihood alternatives to the local population (especially the women-folk). However, with the formalization of the organised trade, natives of Manipur have failed to reap the harvest of success. At present, major share of the trade is undertaken by rich businessmen and members of the Confederation of Indian Industry and Federation of Indian Chamber of Commerce. Thus, in addition to taking away the livelihood alternatives from the natives, policy makers failed to take into account gender sensitive issues as well as failed to acknowledge historical/traditional role of Manipuri women in trade and commerce. This suggest that empowerment of the people by maximizing self-governance and participatory development through grassroots planning, much voiced by policy-makers are void promises. The border trade has not taken into account needs and aspirations of the people. In fact, it has not created greater employment opportunities and expanded choices for people of Manipur. Manipur, as such, remains a transit point and victim of cheap Chinese-made consumer goods. This also means that local handicrafts and products of looms are fighting a hopeless battle against cheap goods being imported, significantly affecting the working class of Manipur.

Militarization of Development Initiatives: Experience from Harnessing Water Power

Blackouts are a regular feature in Manipur. Manipur gets its share of power from the Central Sector Power plants located in the North Eastern Region. The share of power for the State from the Central sector power plants including the shares from the unallocated share of power of the Central Projects is 122.52 MW when the plants are operated at their full capacity. The present requirement of the State is 170 MW during peak hours; whereas the availability of power from Central Sector Power plants varies from 45 MW during summer off peak to 119MW during monsoon peak.[23]

The *Draft Industrial and Investment Policy of Manipur, 2011* states that Manipur is richly endowed with considerable Hydro Power Potential of about 2000 MW, which is sufficient not only to meet the local requirement for domestic and industrial uses but leave surplus for marketing outside. However, barely 108.2 MW has been harnessed in the form of one medium project and micro projects.[24] The Loktak Hydro Electric Project (3×35 MW) commissioned in 1984 is so far the main source of power supply in the State.

The State Power Department has so far identified about a dozen of hydro power potential sites in the State and they are

Box 3.1: Keeping Tradition Alive (Experts)

Stacks of bright hand woven "Phaneks" (wrap-arounds) adorn the small benches in the market. The reflection of the hanging lamps falling on the coloured clothes make them look all the more magical. This is the women's market in Imphal, Manipur, a market totally run and managed by women, historically and culturally crucial, tinted with layers of memories.

So, how did it all begin? As Apanbi, trader of traditional clothes, says, "this market has an age-old history. It has been there from before the colonial period. And always women had played a major role in promoting trade and indigenous products. Hence, the name 'Ima Keithel' (market run by women)."

They've always faced challenges from rival markets, controlled by men. Some time in 1948-1952, some local male merchants even tried to demolish the existing shed. Another major incident occurred in the early 1990s, when the women received an eviction notice from the State urban development authorities.

Targeting a way of Life

An assault on the "Keithel" is not just an assault on a system of trading; it is a systematic attempt to destroy a way of life. All over the Northeast, forces of globalisation and privatisation, backed by the State's hegemony, are ousting indigenous women's markets and production centres. Poverty is being created, intensified and deliberately entrenched. In its new *avatar*, it is feminised poverty that is being sought to be perpetrated. The global market is neither abstract nor intangible as it is often projected. It can be demarcated by real space: physical, economic and cultural. Where such space is already occupied by traditional and indigenous systems and practices, it must be cleared to make possible a smooth entry for the global market.

In Northeastern India, women have traditionally been managing trade and commerce. They are also producers of many goods for consumption, local exchange and even for regional markets. They are the most active conservers of biodiversity (agro, wetland and forest), both through their farming practices, and through their active promotion of the local gastronomic cultures.

These markets are an example of this sophisticated system of trade. The term "market" is highly inadequate to describe what a Keithel is and the role that it plays in the local economy, culture and society. It is a site for the affirmation of women's control over the production, use and management of consumption patterns. It represents the attempt of communities to assert their food sovereignty, economic self-determination and cultural diversity. It is for this reason that the Keithels of Manipur have been under attack through history. Without control over the Keithel, the subjugation of communities that live around it can never be complete.

Ironic Turnaround

During the famous "Nupi Lan" (wars) of Manipur, on three celebrated occasions during the 19th century, the women confronted artillery of the British forces with sticks. The colonial power recognised that this system had to be brought under a more pliable economic system that could be more easily infiltrated. Ironically, the struggle has been acknowledged by the Government of India, which has

(*Contd.*)

built a memorial dedicated to these women. Yet it has not hesitated to replicate the tactics of its predecessor.

The reasons for the State onslaught are primarily because many sites devoted to these markets are located in the centre of towns. Soaring real estate prices make them vulnerable. For neo-liberal market forces, it is difficult to see the land as anything other than a piece of real estate, waiting to be "developed" into shopping malls. They cannot see these as not just hubs of commerce, but also of socio-political processes.

Source: Nilosree Biswas, "Keeping tradition alive", *The Hindu*, 10 September, 2006.

at different stages of implementation. Some of these sites are shown in Table 3.4.

Table 3.4: Potential Sites of Hydro Power in Manipur

Sl. No.	*Name of Project*	*Capacity (MW)*
1.	Loktak Down Stream HE-Project	66
2.	Tipaimukh HE-Project	1500
3.	Pabram HE-Project	2x95
4.	Irang HE-Project	4x15
5.	Tuivai HE-Project	3x17
6.	Nungleiband HE-Project	2x35
7.	Khongnem Chakha HE-Project	2x33.5

Source: Government of Manipur, Draft Industrial and Investment Policy of Manipur, 2011.

The State Government has so far been following the guidelines and policy of Government of India for power generation programmes to be implemented by the Private Sector Units. In addition to the Fiscal and Promotional incentives of the Government of India for participation by Private Sector Institutions/Companies in the generation and supply from generating stations the State Government is making preparation to frame a policy of its own to further facilitate private participation and investment in the field of generation, transmission and distribution. The Government has given top priority consideration on generation to develop hydro power potential as one of the major industries. It has decided to invite private investors in the Generation industry.

The Government of Manipur welcomes private participation in the projects given below[25]:

1. *Pabram HE Project*: The project is located near Tamenglong Khunjao in Tamenglong District, Manipur at a distance of about 21 km. from Tamenglong District Headquarters. It is a storage scheme and aims to utilize the inflow of Barak River. The project envisages construction of a 122m high concrete gravity dam having a gross storage of 921.30m cum.[26] The catchment area of the river at dam site is 2449 sq. km. A head race tunnel having a diameter of 7.5m and 6.5 km long is to be constructed to take the water from the reservoir to the Power House. The proposed Power House shall be having an installed capacity of 190 MW with two units of 95 MW each. The Project has also other components like spillway with a discharging capacity of 12145 cumecs, intake tunnel of 7.5 m dia., a 143 m high surge shaft of 18 m dia. And two penstocks each having 4.4 m dia.[27]

2. *Irang HE Project*: The project site is located near Taobam village on NH-53 in Tamenglong District. It is a storage scheme and envisages construction of a 104m high earthen Dam across Irang River. The power house to be constructed at the toe of the dam shall be having an installed capacity of 60MW with 4 (four) units of 15MW each.[28] Survey and investigation of the project is presently in the advance stage.

3. *Tuivai HE Project*: The project site is located near Dailkhai village in Thanlon Sub-Division of Churachandpur District. It is a storage scheme and aims to utilize the inflow of Tuivai River, a tributary of Barak. The project envisages construction of 110m high earthen dam with a gross storage of 380.80m cum.[29] The proposed power house to be constructed at the toe of the dam shall be having an installed capacity of 51 MW with three units of 17 MW each.[30]

4. *Nungleiband HE Project*: The project is proposed to be taken up near Nungleiband village in Tamenglong District. It is a run off the river scheme and aims to utilise the tail race discharge of existing Loktak HE Project and the inflow of Leimatak River which is a tributary of Barak River. The project envisages construction of a 28m high barrage and 14m long head race tunnel. The power house shall be having an installed capacity of 70 MW with two units of 35 MW each. The annual energy generation is 363.95 MU. The total project cost is Rs. 7200.40 million approximately based on June 2007 price level. The generation cost works out as Rs. 3.30 per unit.[31]

5. *Khongnem Chakha Project*: The project is located near Maram Centre in Senapati District, Manipur. It is at the upper reach of the Barak River. The project envisages construction of a 52 m high concrete gravity dam and 15 km long head race tunnel of 3.5 m diameter.[32] The power house shall be having an installed capacity of 67 MW with two units of 33.5 MW each. Survey and investigation is yet to be started.[33] In addition, the State also has taken up irrigation projects with power generation component, like—

The Militarization Experience: Case of the Tipaimukh Dam

Development initiatives are undertaken through militarization is amply testified by the various dam projects undertaken in Manipur. The attempted construction of the multi-purpose Tipaimukh Dam and dam at Mapithel provides instances of militarization in the name of development, which not only brings in the issue of security and threat to livelihood instances but also environmental hazards and issue of displacement. The Tipaimukh HE Project would have the capacity to generate 1500 MW of power. Civil society organizations have assessed the potential demerits of large hydroelectric projects, since such projects involve dislocation of people, submergence of valuable resources including forests, loss of estuaries and endangered species and adverse impacts on downstream hydrology and siltation. On these grounds, rigid opposition was stalled against the setting up of the 1500mw Tipaimukh project.

Proposed construction of a multipurpose project at Tipaimukh, which was granted notification in 2003, is also case in point. The entire lowland along the banks of three major river courses of Manipur—the Barak, the Irang and the Makru, which runs through the length of Tamenglong district, would be under perpetual threat of submergence (Churchill, 2006: 39). Following Table 3.5 shows the areas likely to be affected by the Tipaimukh Multipurpose Project.

Table 3.5: Areas likely to be affected by the Tipaimukh Multipurpose Project

Area of land likely to be affected (in hectares)	*No. of villages likely to be affected*	*No. of villagers likely to be displaced*	*Area of natural habitat likely to be destroyed (in sq. km)*	*Length of NH 53 likely to be dislocated (in km)*
15,000.00	168.00	30,000.00	300.00	60.00

Source: Compiled from, Laishram Churhill, 2006. Environment, Development and Social Challenges: Scrutinising India's Look East Policy in Manipur. *Alternative Frames* I, III. April–June: 30-46.

However, in August 2008, the Government of Manipur took the decision to deploy heavy security in area where the Tipaimukh multipurpose hydro-electricity project will be established. In other words, Manipur Government and NEEPCO derided voice of the people and attempted to build the dam through militarization of the area. Such as move came against the understanding that militarization is responsible for the chaos and endless conflict in Manipur. Ceaseless employment of force by the State is further empowered by the Armed Forces Special Powers Act, which has robbed away many lives in the State. In other words, India does not respect the rights and dignity of the people, guaranteed by international conventions such as the United Nations Declaration on the Rights of the Indigenous Peoples and United

Nations Declaration of Human Rights. Some civil society organizations feel that what is inherent in the construction of the proposed dam is akin to occupation and annexation of land of the natives.

At present although the construction of the dam is not under progress, Manipur state authorities have opened security posts at seven kilometre intervals along the 99 km stretch of Mon Bahadur Road, which is to be used for movement of materials required for the construction of the controversial dam. Various divisions of Assam Rifles keep a close vigilance and any time the forces can be deployed at the site of construction. At the same time, the forces are used to flush out insurgents from the Churachandpur District adjoining Myanmar and Mizoram. Human rights violation of the civilians with undue "collateral damage" once again is the core issue of concern.

In addition to the proposed construction of the Tipaimukh Dam, the Government of Manipur envisages construction of dams such as Loktak Downstream HE Project (90MW), Irang HE Project (60 MW) and other microhydel projects at Leimakhong (Stage-III), Gelnel (Stage-I) and Tuipokpi, Haipi, Maklang, Iring, Ijai and Tupul 4.50 MW. None of these poposed projects have received environmental clearances.

The Militarization Experience: Case of the Loktak Lake

It is worthwhile to mention the incidence surrounding the Loktak (largest fresh water lake in the North east India and site of the Loktak Hydro Electric Project) protection drive undertaken by the Government of Manipur through the implementation of the Loktak Protection Act, 2006 (amended in 2007). In September 2011, barely 24 hours since serving quit notice, humble houses of impoverished lake (*phumdi*) dwellers were burnt down together with all their belongings by the Loktak Development Authority (LDA).[34]

Voices of resistance emerged against the Loktak Protection Act, 2006 months back before the humble huts were burnt

Box 3.2: Excerpts from Tipaimukh Dam: Development or Destruction by David Buhril

The attempt to secure energy in these fringe geography has already insecure indigenous people who were put at the altar without any democratic consultations. This has severed the the Tipaimukh villagers whose ancestral land and resource were being targeted as urban fodder. With their cultural and identity footprints firmly attached to Tipaimukh, the proposed Tipaimukh dam has come to represent an imperialist, like character that the forgotten people are yet to come to terms with.

The dogged efforts exerted by the Government of Manipur and North East Electric Power Corporation (NEEPCO) to dam Tuiruong (Tipaimukh) and Tuivai rivers for the Tipaimukh Hydro Electric Multipurpose Project has come to represent development aggression. The aggressive character have today been affirmed by the Government of Manipur decision to militarise Tipaimukh. Much before the environmental clearance was given, the Government of Manipur decided to open security posts at seven kilometre intervals along the 99 km stretch of Mon Bahadur Road, which is to be used for movement of materials required for the construction of the controversial dam. A total of 15 posts of the Central Reserve Police Force (CRPF), Border Security Force (BSF) and Indian Reserve Battalion (IRB) will be initially stationed to provide security for the movement of officials of NEEPCO, the implementing agency of the project. Moreover, the Union Government had already promised a Rs. 400 crore security cover for the proposed project. For the military station, villagers of the doom-bound Sipuikawn, which will be submerged by the dam water were made to allot land at the top of the hill. "We heard that they would be coming in anytime soon. They have chosen the highest point of our hill. I think the dam water would not touch them while our village is predicted to go under water", Rorel of Sipuikawn village said.

The uninformed villagers were told that the project was conceived by the Government and that the project would go ahead regardless of their opposition. Tipaimukh villagers were made to feel like squatters on their ancestral land. The overt aggressiveness is seen by many as a tactic to further made the people helpless; to compel them to give up their land for the project to take shape. This has immensely put a pressure on the villagers who were also frequently baited by the promises of contract, job, compensation, employment prospects and promises of everything that is missing in their lives. "For a deprived community who are already suppressed with high-handed policies and decisions, the political motives are not people-centred and there is no trace of us getting the proclaimed benefits. The dam will be the biggest trap in our lives", a mission teacher said.

Apprehension has caught the Tipaimukh villagers imagination in the absence of transparency. The project had once fragmented the fringe society creating a minor class of pro-dam and the left out majority who are totally opposed to the dam. However, slowly, the looming ambiguities that has been playing with their ancestral land has pulled them together with a collective quest for securing their rights and land. This has resulted in the conflict of interest where the State interpretations of development did not seep in easily despite the money spill in the already investment stage that the project has entered.

Source: Classic.kanglaonline.com/index.php?template=kshow&kid=1461&Idoc_Session=02e8bff175f2626479332639933c25b9

down. The Act has been justified on the grounds of heritage, as a fulcrum of ecological balance in the state and most specifically as a biodiversity hot spot. The Act has been implemented within the larger framework of the "Save Loktak Campaign." Consequent upon the implementation of the Act, livelihood of the people who have traditionally been dependent upon the water body have been affected. Government while denying the affected people a place for their voice, which they raised in response to the disturbances to their life, work and deportment (displacement), has also horrendously misrecognised these voices. They are now framed within the volt of state's own language and categorized as anti-development, anti-government and anti-state. In this habitual framing, the victims are now identified as a security threat, not as ones demanding their rightful places. Within this order, also developing is a body of legalities and illegalities. Loktak is now more than a lake. It has already transgressed the nature that it was once lovingly understood with. It has been now metamorphosed into something that closely looks like an economy of "illegality" built around to check anti-government and anti-state elements. Cleaning the Loktak is cleaning these elements off, not about saving a heritage.

The story of despoilation of Loktak begins with the construction of the Loktak Project in 1971 under the control of Ministry of Irrigation and Power, as a Central sector project. The project was handed over to the NHPC six years later and commissioned in 1983 at an estimated cost of Rs.115 crore, with a capacity of 105 MW (3×35 MW). This dam has 'permanently' raised the water level of this wetland and has blocked the natural flow of water to and/or from the wetland, severely altering the hydrologic cycle of a delicately balanced system. Before the construction of the Ithai barrage, the natural dredging process continuously cleared the silt brought down by the various streams and rivers from the valley and the hills. The roots of phumdi and other aquatic vegetation during the lean season touched the bottom. During the monsoon, the water level and the vegetation rose, bringing silt up with it. Much of this silt was drained out through the Manipur River with the current, together with some of the vegetation or Phumdi.

In the post-barrage scenario, the water level is sought to be maintained at a particular level throughout the year, resulting in the silting up of the wetland at an unprecedented rate. Other changes to the floating Phumdi have led to the endangering of native aquatic vegetation, the extinction of native fish species and the thinning and proliferation of the Phumdi, which now covers more than half of the total area of the present water body. Remote sensing studies conducted jointly by the Manipur Remote Sensing Application Centre and the Space Application Centre, Ahmedabad (1999) shows that the area under Phumdi has increased from 10,499 ha in 1990 to 13,506 ha in 1994. Consequently, the water mass has reduced from 15,441 ha in 1990 to 7,875 ha in 1995. According to the Survey of India, prior to the dam, in 1970, the water mass was 4,882 ha, with no indication of seasonal variations. The hydropower multipurpose project had already submersed around 83,000 hectors of cultivable land leaving thousands of farmers unemployed.

Water and Power Consultancy Services Ltd. (WAPCOS), Delhi, a consultant for the Loktak Development Authority (LDA), has pointed out that the rate of siltation has increased due to "jhumming, deforestation and unscientific land-use practices in the catchment areas." The present siltation rate is approximately 336,325 tonnes annually.[35] This, as in the case of most reservoirs, is greater than what was projected during the project's conception. At this rate, the reservoir will reach Dead Storage Level much before the 160 years estimated in Loktak Lift Irrigation Project (Revised), Vol.1, May 1980.

Using various provisions of the Act, Government of Manipur started forcefully evicting the fishermen from their habitats at the Lake in the name of environment protection of the Lake. Within five days starting from November 15,

2011, state forces burnt down around 500 floating huts as a result of which more than 2000 fishermen including women and children became internally displaced people. More than 500 huts were reduced to ashes, fishermen claimed that property worth lakhs of rupees including implements used in fishing such as fishing gears, nets, domestic articles, cloths, and ornaments were lost. The victims were not even allowed to travel to Imphal or other places to voice their grievances. There was no public hearing, peaceful democratic process, nor any workable rehabilitative plan prior to the violent act of eviction. The State announced only a package of Rs. 40,000 as compensation to each family. The fishermen denounced such notice and compensation. They submitted a memorandum to Shri O. Ibobi Singh, the State Chief Minister, requesting to review the order, which was turned down by the Chief Minister himself. Fishermen stated that the order was unacceptable since it could not ensure them any alternative livelihood. They demanded repeal or amendment of Loktak Lake (Protection) Act, 2006 in order to assure their right to fishing and dwelling on the Phumdis, which were practiced by their ancestors since time immemorial.[36] Today, what has emerged is that cleaning the Loktak lake at the cost of livelihood and homestead of the fisherman is nothing but divert water to Loktak Project for more efficient functioning and sanitizing the lake of the insurgents.

Conclusion

Logic of inviting investment in cash strapped economy of Manipur, trade initiatives to uplift the same economy and development initiatives, as we have learned from the experience of Manipur testify that it has harmed the State more than doing her good. In all the initiatives one has failed to look beyond the security perspective. In such a scenario, the proposed India-EU FTA carries the potential of harming the region. And as such, the proposed free trade agreement does not intend to take social, security and human rights issues.

Box 3.3: Experts Demand Relief for Displaced Loktak Fishers' Community (Excerpts)

A one-day discussion on "Contradictions of Ramsar Conventions Standards and Guidelines with Loktak Wetlands Management in Manipur" was organized by the All Loktak Lake Areas Fishermen's Union and All Manipur Thanga People's Welfare Association today at the Conference Hall of Manipur State Central Library, Imphal. Haobijam Kula, General Secretary of All Loktak Lake Areas Fishermen's Union, while deliberating the key note address stated that the present day management of the Loktak Lake has only led to hardship and inconvenience to the indigenous people depending on Loktak wetlands for survival, as testified by the recent arsoning and destruction of the floating huts belonging to the fisherfolk of Loktak Lake.

Dr. Debabrata Roy Laifungbam, Executive Director, CORE said that Loktak Lake, already recognized as wetlands of International importance under the Ramsar Convention and listed in the International Montreaux Record as endangered wetlands has long been managed without recognizing people's, community rights over the use and management of wetlands in Manipur. The present day management of Loktak Wetlands violates the guidelines and standards stipulated by the Ramsar Convention on Wetlands Management, such as the resolution VII.8 and VIII.19 of Ramsar Convention's Conference of contracting parties held in May 1999 at Costa Rica and Spain in November 2002. The efforts of the Loktak Development Authority are more to ensure government control of Wetlands and not for conservation of Loktak Wetlands, he noted.

The Loktak Protection Act, 2006 is more focused on control and administration of wetlands by the government, which is very much evident by the trend of violent arsoning of floating huts in Loktak Lake with the LDA, Manipur Police under the Act. The LPA, 2006 also did not mention the importance of people's participation in wetlands while the Ramsar conventions stipulated that wetlands management should be with due participation of the community depending on the wetlands along with the local and national government and international cooperation, he added. "The LPA, 2006 has become a draconian law, not only anti to the people but also against the spirit of protection of nature itself".

Dr. Laifungbam also said that the classification of Loktak as core and buffer zone is inappropriate as Ramsar Conventions calls for conservation of all parts of the wetlands and not to prioritize on selected and restricted parts of the Lake. The creation of roads and ring bandh inside the Loktak Lake itself is a violation of Ramsar Conventions, Dr. Debabrata asserted.

Yumnam Rupachandra, editor, *ISTV* said that the current state of affairs in Manipur is due to the ineffectiveness of the local authorities, which has long failed to take independent decisions sensitive to people's rights and needs of the people of Manipur. The leaders of Manipur should stop taking decisions impacting on communities rights. It's time to cross check the process of electing people's representatives. It's time for the people of Manipur to unite and question, reflect the trend of development processes introduced in Manipur and media needs to take more responsibility, he added.

(*Contd.*)

Khoirom Loyalakpa, editor, *Naharol Thoudang* said that the current arsoning of floating huts is only to harness financial allocations for counter insurgency purpose in the name of conservation of Loktak Lake.

Later, the participants of the one-day discussion adopted a number of resolutions including the Government of Manipur should provide immediate alternate relief for the 273 affected landless fishermen living on phum huts inside the Loktak Lake for ages and who are currently seeking shelter at Thanga Haoreng Chingyang community hall after displacement due to arson of their floating huts in November 2011 to ensure their reparation and redress. The resolution also includes the fishing community living at Thanga, Karang and other peripheral areas of the Loktak Lake should be allowed to build adequate number of floating huts/phums huts (Khangpokshang) inside the lake so as to provide shelter during storm, heavy rains and hot suns and also to promote the cultural heritage of the people of Manipur. The resolutions also include demand for compensation not less than Rs. three lakh to each affected fishing communities as rehabilitation; provision of land for the 273 landless fisherfolks and that no part of Loktak Lake should be declared as fishery and to demand to formulate Loktak Lake Fisherfolk Rights and Welfare Act among others.

Source: "Experts demand relief for displaced Loktak fishers' community", *The Imphal Free Press*, Imphal, December 18, 2011.

Thus, we find a scenario where goods are dumped into Manipur at the cost of the local producers and artisans, thereby threatening their livelihood. Unemployment is bound to be a dire consequence. At another level, local entrepreneurs and businessmen cannot be part of the competition, given that since colonial times, bulk of the trade has been in the hands of the outsiders, such as the Marwaris. Not only the entry level competition is tough but also sustaining a business in the face of competitors and market dictates (fluctuations, artificial scarcity, procurement method, supply chain etc.) are arts that the local population has not mastered. These are areas, where state intervention is required and protectionism needed to foster local entrepreneurs. Energy sector is where the State Government hopes to attract investment. Obviously this is an area where, EU investors would definitely eye for. But again the matter concern rallies around human security such as environmental consequences, displacement as result of construction of mega dams, and related issues of militarization. Given the record of human rights violation in the state it is pertinent to engage the people *vis-à-vis* the Indian Government and EU, for an approach that can reduce harm.

Notes

1. Institute for Human Development, 2006.
2. *Ibid.*
3. Sachdeva, 2000, *op. cit.*
4. Singh, 2005, *op. cit.*, 149–60.
5. Government of India, "Report of High Level Commission to the Prime Minister, 'Transforming the North east: Tackling Backlogs in Basic Minimum Services and Infrastructural Needs'", Planning Commission: New Delhi, March 7, 1997.
6. *Ibid.*
7. *Ibid.*
8. *Ibid.*
9. The existing Indo-Myanmar Border Trade in the border towns of Moreh and Tamu has already paved the way for a full scale trade between India and Myanmar which would further extend to other adjacent countries, like Thailand, Laos, South West China along the old Burma road and the proposed Trans-Asia Highway and Railway.
10. Government of Manipur, *Draft Industrial Policy of Manipur,* 2011.
11. Government of Manipur, *Industrial Policy of Manipur,* 1996.
12. *Ibid.*
13. Laishram Churchill, "Manipur's Economy: Trajectory and Transformation Before and During the British Period", *Alternative Perspectives,* Vol. III, No. 3, March–June, 2006, p. 23.
14. *Ibid.*, p. 26.
15. Kishan, 2006, *op. cit.*, 55-68.
16. Shukla, *op. cit.*, 1997.
17. World Bank Study 2005, *Voices of the Poor.*
18. Amar Yumnam, "Development Intervention in the North east: A Critique", *Eastern Quarterly,* Vol. 3, Issue III, October-December 2005.
19. Report of the Human Rights Initiatives, 2009.
20. *Ibid.*
21. *Ibid.*
22. *Ibid.*
23. *Ibid.*
24. *Ibid.*
25. *Ibid.*
26. *Ibid.*

27. *Ibid.*
28. *Ibid.*
29. *Ibid.*
30. *Ibid.*
31. *Ibid.*
32. *Ibid.*
33. *Ibid.*
34. Yenning, "Crackdown on Phumdi Dwellers: An Ugly Face of Developmental Terrorism", *The Sangai Express*, Sunday, January 1, 2012.
35. *Ibid.*
36. *Ibid.*

4

Extractive Industry, Oil and Natural Gas Sector and the EU

A three-day maiden visit in May 2012 by a Delegation of Ambassadors from European countries to Nagaland sent shock waves at least to quarters. The Union Home Ministry was upset over the European members' visit as the delegates have not taken any security clearance from it and has asked the Ministry of External Affairs to explain its "unilateral" decision to give clearance to the visit. The Home Ministry was upset over the meeting of diplomats with Naga civil society groups and political parties on the ground that the Naga political issue would be internationalised.[1] On the other hand, civil society organisizations in region working in the areas of livelihood and human security viewed the visit as a silent manoeuvre of assessment of potential investment, as the India-EU FTA dialogue is already in progress. Moreover, recently, the United States of America has taken initiatives for investment plan in the region. In February 2012, the United States Ambassador Peter Burleigh said, "trade missions including American companies from his country will visit the north eastern region soon to explore possibility of investment in key sectors." He also said, "We are open to exploring virtually any area for investment."[2] Furthermore, in the last few years, the North east has become a destination of MNCs for exploration and drilling of oil. Reliant Energy is a case in point. In addition to energy from water harnessing extractive industry and oil and natural gas are potential sectors for investment from the European Union.

Issues related with mining and exploration and drilling of oil and natural gas are such ventures undermine the traditional customary laws on land use and violates environmental and forest laws of India and other international human rights and Indigenous People's standards. Further, there are related issues of resettlement, protection of Indigenous Peoples and promoting sustainable development. As such, any free trade agreement should be sensitive to such matters and Government should work out safeguards for the local population and resources. It shall be shown in the following sections, such as the case pertaining to Odisha and Meghalaya, in the case of mining, Union laws prevails over State legislations and MNCs come out victorious. The same is the case with oil and natural gas exploration and drilling in the case of Manipur.

Mining and Mineral Ores

The Draft Industrial and Investment Policy of Manipur, 2011 places mining (extractive industry) as an area of potential investment. However, it is silent on oil and natural gas. Further, other than giving an estimate of available deposit, unlike the case of hydel projects, it has not made any project estimates. Nevertheless, these are areas where the State is looking for investments and returns. Minerals in Manipur are mainly confined to certain types of rocks such as ophiolite suite, Oceanic Pelagic Sediment (OPS) and melanges in the Ophiolite Belt. Amongst these, chromite, limestone and serpentinites (as dimensional stone) are important for immediate exploitation. Other minerals are PGE/PGM (platinum group elements/platinum group minerals), idocrase, rock salt etc.

Chromite Deposits

The chromite deposits of Manipur fall in the third category of Indian chromite associated with the Tertiary Ophiolite Formation.[3] The GSI and the State Geology and Mining Division have recorded a number of chromite occurrences of metallurgical and refractory grades from the ophiolite belt of Manipur in Ukhrul and Chandel districts bordering Myanmar. Chromites occur as floats on the surface and *in situ* pods of varying dimensions. These chromites are found as massive boulders, blocks, tabular bodies as well as nodular masses within the altered ultramafics.[4] Some are also found as disseminated type. These belong to the Alpine Type Podiform Chromite. There is possibility of occurrences of deep-seated chromite in this belt. Intensive searching and exploration using geophysical and drilling inputs are necessary. Preparation for intensive search is going on and will be completed soon.[5] Availability of chromite deposits in Manipur is given in Table 4.1.

Table 4.1: Chrome Deposit

Sl. No.	Name of deposit	District	Probable reserve	Grade	CaO%
1.	Phangrai	Ukhrul	77,400 tonnes upto 1 m depth	Metallurgical and Refractory	42.92 to 50.27%
2.	Hangkau	do	66,000 tonnes upto 1 m depth	do	24.6 to 30.30 (Cr_2 2%)
3.	Gamnom	do	1,68,900 tonnes upto 1m depth	do	39.11 to 50.00%
4.	Nampisha	do	1,25,200 tonnes	do	40.1 to 55.0%
5.	Sirohi	do	13,500 tonnes	do	40 to 57%
6.	Kwatha	Chandel	66,000 tonnes upto 1 m depth	do	42.92 to 53.29%
7.	Khudengthabi	do	28,500 upto 1 m depth	do	45 to 53%

Source: Government of Manipur, *Draft Industrial and Investment Policy of Manipur, 2011.*

Seven Sisters Post, Kolkota reported on May 10, 2012 that scores of mining companies from mainland states have lined up exploration drilling plans for chromite in Manipur but are yet to start off for lack of security. Companies such as Visa and Ananda Ferro Alloys, which are based in Odisha and claimed to "very experienced in extraction and processing" of chromite has plans for exploratory drilling in Ukhrul district but has been delayed as "The State Government is promising us protection but there are so many rebel groups operating in the State and we are not sure how to get started."[6]

Earlier the move to extract natural resources including chromite from the Phangrei range near Shiroi peak in Manipur's Ukhrul district has evoked opposition from the human rights bodies, besides leaving certain questions unanswered. Tangkhul bodies including the Naga People's Movement for Human Rights (NPMHR), Ukhrul Chapter in particular, is monitoring the issue in association with the affected villagers. "Besides our activities on educating human rights, we are now focusing on issues relating to the mining activities in our region."[7] NPMHR also sharply reacted to the assurance made by the State leaders in a Business Summit outside the State to provide security for the investors who wish to come to Manipur. According to the sources, one Odisha mining company is reportedly all set to start mining activities in the Phangrei range which comes under the jurisdiction of Sehai village authority in order to extract Chromite despite the objection from the villagers and others also not happy with the government's move, sources added.

Limestone Deposits

Cement and Steel Melt Shop (SMS) grades of limestone are found in the lensoidal bodies of melanges in the west and in the Oceanic Pelagic Sediment (OPS) in the east of Ophiolite belt of Manipur in Ukhrul and Chandel districts.[8] Limestones are mainly massive with a few fissile at the periphery. They occur as bouldery outcrops and bedded lensoids of varying dimensions. These limestones can also be used in lime burning industries. The important limestone deposits are mainly reported from three linear melange bands in the west of Ophiolite belt in Disang sediments. There are more than 85 small limestone deposits in the ophiolite belt of Manipur.

Some of the important limestone deposits in Manipur are given in Table 4.2 below.

Table 4.2: Limestone Deposits in Manipur

Sl. No.	*Name of deposit*	*District*	*Probable Reserve*	*Grade*	*CaO%*
1.	Ukhrul	Ukhrul	4630000 tonnes	Cement and SMS Grade	43 to 44
2.	Hundung North	do	501000 tonnes	do	44.3 to 50
3.	Hundung South	do	170000 tonnes	do	50.65
4.	Mava	do	36000 tonnes	do	50.65
5.	Phungyar	do	1532000 tonnes	do	48.70
6.	Meiring	do	5760000 tonnes	do	49-50
7.	New Paoyi	do	256000 tonnes	do	47.25
8.	Khangkhui	do	260000 tonnes	do	47.74
9.	Narum	do	158000 tonnes	do	47.86

Source: Government of Manipur, *Draft Industrial and Investment Policy of Manipur, 2011.*

Serpentinites

Serpentinites occur extensively in Chandel and Ukhrul districts within the Ophiolite Belt of Manipur extending over an area of 1100 sq.km. (about 110 km. long and 5-15 km. wide).[9] The belt trends NE-SW from south of Moreh in Chandel District to north-east of Tushom in Ukhrul District up to Nagaland border and technically overlies the Disang sediments on its west and is interlayered with Oceanic Pelagic Sediments.

Serpentinites are also commercially known as "Green Marble." It, like granite and marble, can be processed into monuments, tiles, slabs and other building blocks. It is considered that Serpentinite of Manipur has a huge market potential, both as finished products and in raw forms, both within India and outside. So far Manipur is concerned, it could become the most important mineral industry generating large scale employment and appreciable export earning.[10]

PGE/PGM and Associated Sulphides

The Arakan-Chin belt extending between the Andaman Islands and the North East India corresponds to a trench-arc up-thrust of the Middle Cenozoic. Small ultramafic bodies are associated with these elongated fold belt. The belt transects the eastern part of Manipur where it covers an area of about 100 km by 15 km.[11] Occurrences of chromite, nickel, PGM and Copper Sulphides have been found along this ophiolite belt in Myanmar, and it is highly probable that the same mineralisations can be found in the Manipur section of the belt (BRGM-France). The Geological Survey of India (GSI) has also reported presence of some PGE/PGM in some chromite and serpentinite samples from Kwatha, Chandel district (20 and 90 ppb) and Phangrai (Ukhrul district).[12] The GSI has further viewed that trace metals like Ni, Co, V, Cu, Cr, Sr, As, Mo, Sn, Mn, Ba, Ti, Zr; precious metals like Au, Ag, PGE (by replacing Cr, V, Ti, Al); and REE like Ce, Ga, La could be enriched in selected locales/horizons in the pelagic sediments. High concentration of Nickel (up to 74,000 ppm) in the soil above the ultramafite was indicated by the GSI in the areas of Gamnom to Ningthi, Ukhrul District, Manipur.[13] The geochemical prospecting also indicated the increase in nickel concentration near the soil-rock contact. Two sulphide mineralisations were also located at Nampisha and Yentem ophiolite suites by the Department of Geology and Mines (DGM). The State DGM has initiated actions to take up the exploration at some selected blocks in technical collaboration with the G.S.I.[14]

Issues Related with Mines and Mineral Ores in India

In India, the State Governments are the owner of minerals

located within the boundaries of the State concerned. Although mineral wealth vests with the State Government, yet the subject of regulation of Mines and Minerals development is covered under 7th Schedule to the Constitution of India. Rule making powers in respect of minor minerals have been delegated to the States under section 15 of this Act.

In accordance with Article 297 of the Constitution, the Central Government is the owner of the minerals underlying the ocean within the territorial waters or the Exclusive Economic Zone of India. In this connection, entry at serial No. 23 of List II (State list) to the Constitution provides that "Regulation of mines and mineral development subject to the provisions of List I with respect to regulation and development under the control of the Union", are within the purview of States while entry at serial No. 54 of List I states that "Regulation of mines and mineral development to the extent to which such regulation and development under the control of the Union is declared by Parliament by law to be expedient in the public interest" shall be within the purview of the Central Government. In pursuance to entry at serial No. 54 of List I, Parliament has passed legislation titled "The Mines and Minerals (Development and Regulation) Act 1957" as Central Act (No. 67 of 1957).

The State Governments grant the mineral concessions for all the minerals located within the boundary of the State, under the provisions of the Mines and Minerals (Development and Regulation) Act 1957 (MMDR) and Mineral Concession Rules, 1960 (MCR) framed thereunder. Under the provisions of the MMDR Act 1957 and MCR, 1960, prior approval of the Central Government is required in the following cases:

- Granting mineral concessions in respect of minerals specified in the First Schedule to the Mines and Minerals (Development and Regulation) Act 1957.
- Granting areas under prospecting licence and mining lease to a person in excess of limits prescribed under Section 6(1) (a) and Section 6(1) (b) of the Act.

- Imposing special condition(s) in mining lease under Rule 27(3), in prospecting licence under Rule 14(3) and in reconnaissance permit under Rule 7(3) of Mineral Concession Rules, 1960 over and above the conditions prescribed in MCR, 1960.
- Granting mineral concession in an area previously reserved by the Government, or previously held under a mineral concession, without first notifying the same by relaxing the provisions of Rule 59(1) under Rule 59(2) of MCR, 1960.
- Revision of any order made by State Government with respect to any mineral except a minor mineral. (Section 30 of MMDR Act).
- Relaxation of Rules in special cases under Section 31 of the Act, keeping in view the interest of mineral development.

There are three kinds of mineral concessions, viz. Reconnaissance Permit (RP), Prospecting Licence (PL) and Mining Lease (ML). RP is granted for preliminary prospecting of a mineral through regional, aerial, geophysical or geochemical surveys and geological mapping. The RP for any mineral or prescribed group of associated minerals is granted for 3 years and for a maximum area of 5,000 sq. kms, to be relinquished progressively. After 2 years, the area should be reduced to 1,000 sq. kms or 50 per cent of the area granted, whichever is less. At the end of 3 years, area held under an RP should be reduced to 25 sq. kms. In a State, a person can be granted a maximum area of 10,000 sq. kms under RP subject to the condition that area in a single RP does not exceed 5000 sq. kms. A RP holder has preferential right to obtain PL(s) in the area concerned.

Prospecting Licence (PL) is granted for undertaking operations for the purpose of exploring, locating or proving mineral deposit. A PL for any mineral or prescribed group of associated minerals is granted for a maximum period of 3 years. A PL can be renewed in such a manner that the total period for which a PL is granted does not exceed 5 years. In a State, a person can be granted a maximum area of 25 sq. kms in one or more PLs, but if the Central Government is of the opinion that in the interest of development of any mineral it is necessary to do so, the maximum area limit can be relaxed. A PL holder has preferential right to obtain ML in the area concerned.

Mining Lease (ML) is granted for undertaking operations for winning any mineral. A ML for any mineral or prescribed group of associated minerals is granted for a minimum period of 20 years and a maximum period of 30 years. A ML can be renewed for periods not exceeding 20 years each. In a State, a person can be granted a maximum area of 10 sq. kms in one or more MLs, but if the Central Government is of the opinion that in the interest of development of any mineral it is necessary to do so, the maximum area limit can be relaxed.

In pursuance of the reforms initiated by the Government of India in July 1991 in fiscal, industrial and trade regimes, the National Mineral Policy was announced in March 1993. The National Mineral Policy recognized the need for encouraging private investment, including foreign direct investment and for attracting state-of-the-art technology in the mineral sector. Further, the policy stressed that the Central Government, in consultation with the State Governments, shall continue to formulate legal measures for the regulation of mines and the development of mineral resources to ensure basic uniformity in mineral administration so that the development of mineral resources keeps pace, and is in consonance with the national policy goals.

In furtherance of the objective of the National Mineral Policy, the MMDR Act 1957 has been amended twice in 1994 and 1999. The Mineral Concession Rules, 1960 (MCR) and the Mineral Conservation and Development Rules, 1988 (MCDR), framed under the MMDR Act 1957 have also been modified. Salient features of the amended mining legislation are as follows:

1. There is no restriction on foreign equity holding in mining sector companies registered in India.
2. There is a greater stability of tenure of mineral concessions, since the minimum period of a mining lease is twenty years and a maximum period of thirty years. A mining lease may be renewed for a period not exceeding twenty years and may again be renewed for a period not exceeding twenty years in respect of minerals specified in Part C of the First Schedule to the Act. In respect of minerals specified in Part A and B of the First Schedule to the Act such renewal may be granted with the previous approval of the Central Government. The period of prospecting licence now is three years, with possibility of renewal for a further period of two years.
3. Thirteen minerals like iron ore, manganese ore, chrome ore, sulphur, gold, diamond, copper, lead, zinc, molybdenum, tungsten, nickel and platinum group of minerals which were reserved exclusively for exploitation by the public sector, have now been thrown open for exploitation by the private sector.
4. With the 1999 Amendment, a concept of reconnaissance operations, as a stage of operation distinct from and prior to actual prospecting operations, was introduced. The period of reconnaissance permit is three years. A reconnaissance permit holder enjoys preferential right for grant of prospecting licence.
5. Area restrictions notified for reconnaissance permit, prospecting licence and mining lease have been made applicable state-wise, instead of the country as a whole.
6. In 1994, fifteen minerals were removed from the list of minerals included in the First Schedule to the MMDR Act 1957. With further amendments in 1999, the mineral limestone was deleted from the First Schedule, and permission of the Central Government

is now required for grant of mining lease, prospecting licence, and reconnaissance permit in respect of only ten non-fuel and non-atomic minerals. These minerals are asbestos, bauxite, chrome ore, copper ore, gold, iron ore, lead, manganese ore, precious stones and zinc.

7. State Governments have been delegated powers to grant mineral concessions even for areas which are not compact or contiguous.
8. State Governments have been empowered to permit amalgamation of two or more adjoining mining leases.
9. State Governments have been empowered to renew prospecting licences/mining leases in respect of specified minerals listed in Part C of the First Schedule, and approval of Central Government is not necessary.
10. State Governments have been delegated powers to approve mining plans in respect of 29 non-metallic/ industrial minerals in case of open cast mines.
11. A time limit of ninety days has been prescribed for the Indian Bureau of Mines and the State Governments to convey the decision on mining plans submitted for approval.
12. Time limits have been prescribed for conveying a decision on applications for mineral concessions, viz. six months for reconnaissance permits, nine months for prospecting licences and twelve months for mining leases.

The procedure for grant of mineral concessions is that all such applications are received and processed in the Directorate of Mines. The application which is received is required to be acknowledged in the prescribed form. The application is thereafter sent to the draughtsman and surveying section to ascertain the availability of the area. After doing the needful, the case is further processed by the dealing hand. If any deficiencies are noticed in the matter of submission of documents as required under the law or as decided by the competent authority, the same are brought to the notice of the applicant for rectification. References are also made to Revenue and Forest Department to ascertain their views on the suitability of the site from the point of public nuisance or forestry angle. The area is also inspected by a geologist of this Directorate to ascertain the suitability of the area from mineral potential point of view including the possible adverse effects arising from prospecting or mining activity. If the area involved is a forest land the case is processed for clearance under Section 2 of FCA if the state government agrees in principle to grant the prospecting licence/mining lease. Clearance under Section 2 of FCA 1980 involves a detailed proposal from the applicant in terms of Forest Conservation Rules and the guidelines prescribed by Ministry of Environment. The applicant is also directed to obtain environmental clearance in terms of EIA Notification dated 14/09/2006.

Irrespective of the above scrutiny and action under FCA, if required, the application is also processed for obtaining a prior approval of the Ministry of Mines, Government of India, if the mineral involved is listed in Schedule I to the Act 1957. After obtaining the prior approval of the Ministry of Mines, Government of India as well Ministry of Environmental Forest, Government of India (where forest land is involved) and the environmental clearance, the case is put up for approval of the State Government. After the issue of the order of grant by the State Government, the area applied for grant of mineral concession is surveyed and demarcated on the ground. A plan is prepared by the surveyor which is signed by the surveyor, the Senior Geologist and the Director and kept in the file as the original document. A true copy of the plan is prepared by the draughtsman, which forms a part of the lease deed document. The applicant is thereafter called upon to effect the payment towards security deposit as well as expenses involving survey, issue of certified copy of plan. A lease deed is thereafter executed at Government level.

Entry 23 of the State List relates to "Regulation of mines and mineral development." However, it is expressly subject to the provisions of the Union List with respect to regulation and development under the control of the Union. Entry 54 of the Union List provides for "Regulation of mines and mineral development to the extent to which such regulation and development under the control of the Union is declared by Parliament by law to be expedient in the public interest." It is significant that Entry 23 of List II has not been made subject to any specific Entry of List I. This means that apart from Entry 54, there are other Entries in List I which may, to an extent, overlap and control, the field of Entry 23 of List II.

The Constitutional arrangements regarding the regulation of Mines and Minerals Development are generally on the lines of Government of India Act, 1935, except that the Entry relating to "Oil fields" has been dealt within a separate Entry, of the Union List in the Constitution (Entry 53 List I).

Parliament has enacted the Mines and Minerals (Regulation and Development) Act, 1957 (MMRD Act) to "provide for regulation of mines and the development of minerals under the control of the Union" in public interest.

Conflicts do arise as to how much of the field of Entry 23 of List II has been taken over by Parliament by enacting the MMRD Act, 1957 by virtue of Entry 54 of List I. Conflicts can also arise when States impose taxes under Entries 18, 49 and 50 of List II. The Constitutional position with regard to Entries on regulation of mines and minerals development and the related Entries in List I and II, therefore, needs to be examined. The Supreme Court has considered these points in a number of reported cases.

The power of the State legislature under Entry 23 has been made subject to the provisions of List I with respect to regulation and development under the control of the Union. Parliament enacted the MMRD Act. A question arose in regard to the extent of the legislative power of the State following an enactment under Entry 54 of List I. It was held by the Supreme Court:

> "The jurisdiction of the State Legislature under Entry 23 is subject to the limitations imposed by the latter part of the Entry. If Parliament by its law has declared that regulation and development of mines should in public interest be under the control of the Union, to the extent of such declaration the jurisdiction of the State Legislature is excluded. In other words, if a Central Act has been passed which contains a declaration by Parliament as required by Entry 54, and if such declaration covers the field occupied by the impugned Act, the impugned Act, will be *ultra vires* not because of any repugnance between the two statutes but because the State Legislature has no jurisdiction to pass a law. The limitations imposed by the latter part of Entry 23 is a limitation on the legislative competence of the State Legislature itself."

The findings in this case have been followed in other cases. In a subsequent case, the Supeme Court held:

> "Subject to the provisions of List I, the power of the State to enact Legislation on the topic of "mines and minerals development" is plenary. To the extent to which the Union Government had taken under "its control", "the regulation and development of minerals" under Entry 54 of List I so much was withdrawn from the ambit of the power of the State Legislature under Entry 23 of List II and legislation of the State which had rested on the existence of power under that Entry would, to the extent of the "control", be superseded or be rendered ineffective; for here we have a case not of mere repugnancy between the provisions of the two enactments but of denudation or deprivation of State legislative power by the declaration which Parliament is empowered to make under Entry 54 of List I and has made. The Central Act 67 of 1957 covered the entire field of minerals

> development that being the "extent" to which Parliament had declared by law that it was expedient that the Union should assume control."

The result, therefore, of Parliament having occupied the entire field is that the State legislature thereafter lacks legislative competence and consequentially, executive authority in regard to regulation and development of mines and minerals. Therefore, where a law is attributable in pith and substance to Entry 23 of List II, it would not be valid in as much as Parliament has occupied the entire field.

States have legislative competence with respect to land and connected matters under Entry 18 of List II and regarding taxes on lands and buildings under Entry 49 of List II. Conflicts have arisen in the matter of levies under Entries 18, 49 and 50 of List II on the ground that they impinge upon Entry 54 of List I. These Entries should also be read with Entry 54 of List I. The State Legislatures' competence is not taken away unless it is shown that in pith and substance the enactment relates to Entry 23 of List II. Dealing with the validity of demand for payment of land cess under Sections 78 and 79 of the Madras District Boards Act (1920), the Supreme Court held that these Sections had nothing to do with the development of mines and mineral or their regulation because the proceeds of the land cess were to be used for providing amenities to the people of the area like education, health etc. It was also observed that the land cess was not a tax or mineral right but was in pith and substance a tax on lands under entry 49 of List II.

Entry 50 of List II relates to taxes on mineral rights. However, this has been made expressly subject to any limitations imposed by Parliament, by law, relating to mineral development. Taxes under Entry 50 of List II do not include royalty and cess.

The MMRD Act 1957 mainly deals with general restrictions on prospecting and mining operations and the rules and procedures for regulating grants of prospecting licences and mining leases. Section 2 of the Act makes a declaration that it is expedient in the public interest that the Union should take under its control the regulation of mines and the development of minerals to the extent provided in the said Act. In Section 3, the words "Minerals", "Mineral Oils", "Minor Minerals" have been separately defined. State Governments are competent to give licences for prospecting and for granting mining leases. The Act specifically provides that in the case of minerals included in the First Schedule to the Act, the State Governments shall not grant or renew, prospecting licences or mining leases without the prior permission of the Union Government. Sections 4 to 12 of the Act deal with the conditions and procedures and other allied matters regarding the prospecting or mining operations under licence or lease. Sections 13 and 13A deal with the rule making power of the Central Government.

It is, however, significant that Section 14 provides that Sections 4 to 13 of the Act shall not apply to minor minerals. Further, Section 15 provides that the State Government's may by notification in the Official Gazette make rule for regarding grant of quarry-lease, mining-lease or other mineral concessions in respect of minor minerals and for the purposes connected therewith. A combined reading of Sections 4 to 13 and Sections 14, 15 and 18 show that while Parliament's enactment (viz. the MMRD Act) has occupied the entire field, it has specifically exempted minor minerals from the application of Sections 4 to 12 and has also empowered the State Governments in respect of minor minerals.

The Odisha Case

In December 1952, the Legislature of the State of Odisha passed the Odisha Mining Areas Development Fund Act. The Act received assent of the Governor. Rules were also duly notified under the Act.

The Administrative Officer concerned with the enforcement of the Act called upon the petitioners to submit the monthly returns for the assessment of the cess. Subsequently, a warning was issued for non-submission of the returns and threatening prosecution under Section 9 of the Act. The petitioners, therefore, filed a petition challenging, *inter alia*, the validity of the Act.

The validity of the Act was challenged on several grounds. One of the grounds was that the State Legislature had no jurisdiction under Entry 23 of List II of the Seventh Schedule of the Constitution since that Entry is subject to provisions of List I with respect to Regulation and Development under the control of the Union; that is Entry 54 of List I. The Court held that a combined reading of Entry 54 of List I and Entry 23 of List II had the following effect:

> The jurisdiction of the State Legislature under Entry 23 is subject to the limitations imposed by the latter part of the Entry. If Parliament by its law has declared that regulation and development of mines should, in public interest, be under the control of the Union, to the extent of such declaration, the jurisdiction of the State Legislature is excluded. In other words, if a Central Act has been passed which contains a declaration by Parliament as required by Entry 54, and if such declaration covers the field occupied by the Impugned Act, the Impugned Act will be *ultra vires* not because of any repugnance between the two statutes but because the State Legislature has no jurisdiction to pass a law. The limitations imposed by the latter part of Entry 23 is a limitation on the legislative competence of the State Legislature itself.

The above Company, incorporated under the Indian Companies Act, was working in the Manganese Mine in the State of Odisha under the lease granted by that State under the provisions of Mines and Minerals (Development and Regulation) Act, 1948, i.e. Central Act 53 of 1948 and the Rules framed therefrom. While so, the Legislature of State of Odisha passed an act called the Odisha Mining Areas

Development Fund Act, 1952 [the same Act was under challenge in *Hingir-Rampur Coal Co.* vs. *State of Odisha* [1961 (2) ACR 537]. The fee under this Act which became due between July 1951 and March 1952 became the subject matter of litigation. A demand was made from the Company. The Company filed a petition before the High Court impugning the legality of the demand and claimed certain assets. The writ petition was allowed by the High Court.

The question arose whether the Mines and Minerals (Development and Regulations) Act, 1948 which is a Central Act has rendered the Odisha Act ineffective. The Supreme Court held as follows:

> Subject to the provisions of List I, the power of the State to enact Legislation on the topic of "mines and mineral development" is plenary. To the extent to which the Union Government had taken under "its control", "the regulation and development of minerals" under Entry 54 of List I so much was withdrawn from the ambit of the power of the State Legislature under Entry 23 of List II and legislation of the State which had rested on the existence of power under that Entry would, to the extent of that "control", be superseded or be rendered ineffective, for here we have a case not of mere repugnancy between the provisions of the two enactments but of a denudation or deprivation of State legislative power by the declaration which Parliament is empowered to make under Entry 54 of List I and has made. The Central Act 67 of 1957 covered the entire field of mineral development, that being the "extent" to which Parliament had declared by law that it was expedient that the Union should assume control.[15]

Relying on the provisions of Section 18(1) which cast a duty upon Union Government "to take all such steps as may be necessary for the conservation and development of minerals in India" and "for that purpose the Central Government may, by notification, make such rules as it may deem fit", it was contended that the entire field of mineral development including the provision of amenities to workmen employed in the mines, vested with the Union Government. The Court was inclined to agree to this contention but held that this position has been concluded by its decision in *Hingir-Rampur Coal Co.* vs. *State of Odisha.*[16]

The appellant's father had obtained a mining lease from the Government of Tamil Nadu. He was permitted to work on the mines and mine the ore in the leased property. It is material to point out that under the lease, the lessee was bound to pay certain rent per year if he used the land for the extraction of iron ore and higher amount if he used the land for other purpose. Besides, he also bound himself to pay certain royalty per tonne of iron ore if the ore was used for extraction or if the iron ore was used for any other purpose for sale at the rate of Re. 1 per tonne (or a higher amount). In addition, there was a stipulation that there was a payment for surface rent.

To raise finance for carrying out local administration in the District Board, several taxes are leviable. Among them, Section 78 of the Madras Distribution Act of 1920 imposes a land cess on lands in the State.

After his father's death, two notices were issued on the appellant demanding payment of the land cess by the District Board for the years 1952-54 and 1955-57 and threatening action in the event of non-payment. The appellant challenged the validity of the notices in the High Court of Andhra Pradesh. The Petition was dismissed. The matter came in appeal before the Supreme Court. One of the contentions was that with the passing of Mines and Minerals (Development and Regulation) Act, 1957, the land cess that could be levied under the District Board Act must be exclusive of royalty under the mining lease.

It was held that there was no connection between regulations and development of mines and minerals dealt with in the Central Act of 1957 and the levy and collection of land cess for which the provision was made by Sections 78 and 79 of the District Boards Act. Therefore, there was no scope at all for the argument that there was anything common in between the District Board's Act and Central Act of 1957 so as to require a detailed examination of these enactments for discovering whether there was any overlapping.

It was further held that land cess imposed by the Madras District Board Act was in truth a tax on land as per Entry 49 of State List and not a tax on minerals under Entry 50 of State List.

The Court also relied on its earlier decisions AIR 1961 SC 459 (Hingir-Rampur Coal Co. *vs.* State of Odisha and AIR 1964 SC 1284—State of Odisha *vs.* M.A. Tullock and Company).[17]

The appellant was the transferee of a lease-hold right, the lessor being one Babu Bijan Kumar Pande. The rent accruing on the lease was deposited up to September 1965.

On coming into force of the Bihar Land Reforms Act, 1950, the lessor Babu Bijan Kumar Pande ceased to have any interest from the date of vesting of the property in the State of Bihar because as per provisions of that Act, the State of Bihar was deemed to be the new lessor.

In its capacity as the new lessor, the rent and royalty etc. in respect of mining and minerals irrespective of the date on which the lease was granted were to be paid by all categories of lessees to the State of Bihar according to the rates given in the rules framed under Bihar Act referred to above. A demand was made according to these rules which became the subject matter of controversy.

The main question that came up for consideration before the Supreme Court was the effect of the combined reading of Entry 54 of the Union List and Entry 23 of the State List of the Seventh Schedule to the Constitution. The Court held:

> [....] it is open to Parliament to declare that it is expedient in the public interest that the control should

> rest in the Central Government. To what extent such a declaration can go is for the Parliament to determine and this must be commensurate with the public interest. Once this declaration is made and extent laid down, the subject of legislation to the extent laid down becomes an exclusive subject for legislation by Parliament. Any legislation by the State after such declaration and trenching upon the field disclosed in the declaration must necessarily be unconstitutional because that field is abstracted from the legislative competence of the State Legislature."[18]

The Court also relied upon its own decisions in *Hingir-Rampur Coal Company* vs. *State of Odisha* (AIR 1961 SC 459) and State of Odisha *vs.* M.A. Tulloch & Co. (AIR 1964 SC 1284). The Court further held:

> "These two cases binding and apply here. Since, the Bihar Legislature amended the Land Reforms Act after coming into force of Act 67 of 1957, the declaration in the latter Act would carve out a field to the extent provided in that Act and to that extent Entry 23 would stand cut down. To sustain the amendment, the State must show that the matter is not covered by the Central Act. The other side must, of course, show that the matter is already covered and there is no room for legislation."[19]

Lafarge Limestone Mining Imbroglio in Meghalaya

Lafarge Surma Cement (LSC) Project was one of the first project of South Asia Sub-regional Economic Cooperation (SASEC) and was promoted and claimed by ADB's former President Tadao Chino as one that visualize ADB's dream of borderless Asia.[20] This transnational project involved a cement plant in Chhatak in Sunamganj district of Bangladesh while the raw materials (limestone) were being sourced from its captive plant in Khasi area of Meghalaya state. LUML (Lafarge Umiam Mining Pvt. Ltd., a French-Spanish joint venture) had been mining the lime stone quarry area spread over 100 hectares. Lafarge and Spanish cement producer Cementos Mollins had set-up the state-of-the-art fully integrated cement plant at Chhatak with a captive power plant of 300 MW. In 2001, the Bangladesh High Commissioner and then Indian Foreign Secretary Lalit Mansingh had singed an agreement for uninterrupted supply of raw material to the plant from the mines in Meghalaya. For the French cement giant Lafarge, the project involved an estimated amount of US$255 million.

Despite Asian Development Bank (ADB)'s call for poverty reduction, sustainable development and respect of indigenous peoples' rights, there are glaring cases of how their involvement in LSC has resulted just the opposite. The project has led to massive takeover of Indigenous People's land of the Khasi People of Meghalaya in North East India, destruction of forest areas which was used for traditional rice cultivation and also other seasonal vegetations and medical plants. The Blasting of hills and forests have caused physical changes leading to artificial changes in water flow regimes, subsequently impact on other aspects of human daily activities.[21]

The LSC project has also seriously undermined the traditional customary laws on land use and violated environmental and forest laws of India and other international human rights and Indigenous Peoples standards.[22] ADB did not apply any of its safeguard policies, concerning Resettlement, on protection of Indigenous Peoples and promoting sustainable development. The application of Accountability Mechanism also has been blocked due to certain clauses in the Mechanism. Rather, ADB relied on World Banks policies, without addressing clear cut accountability and monitoring mechanisms.[23]

Lafarge entered into legal wrangle on account of stiff opposition from civil society bodies, the Shella Action

Committee. In February 2010, a three judge special bench headed by Chief Justice K.G. Balakrishnan ordered for a complete halt of mining in East Khasi Hill District till March 19, 2010. It further directed for pricing of the piled up material already mined at the prevailing market price. The Court passed the order taking into account two grounds. First, the allegation of tribal land was being transferred to the French company's subsidiary and then mortgaged to foreign banks for raising a loan of US $153 million.[24] It was pointed out to the Court that land under mining in Shella in Meghalaya was sold to Lum Mawshun Mineral Pvt. Ltd. which was further transferred in 2006 to Lafarge Umiam Mining Pvt. Ltd. (LUMPL). This land has now been mortgaged to Lafarge Surma Cement which is a joint venture of French cement giant and Cementos Mentus Spanish Company.

Second, not only was the eco-fragile area opened up without the mandatory forest clearance, the raw material was being sent to Bangladesh at the cost price depriving India of a huge revenue due from customs and other duties.[25] The Court, remarked, "It is a very serious issue. Both issue of mortgagee of land to foreign banks and mining in eco-fragile areas have to be answered."[26]

However, in July 8, 2011, literally injecting a fresh lease of life at LUMPL, which was loosing approximately US$1 million every month, the Supreme Court of India lifted an interim stay that opposed mining activities in Meghalaya. It allowed LUMPL, to resume limestone mining in Nongtrai, East Khasi Hills, Meghalaya.[27] The SC dismissed a series of petitions filed by Shella Action Committee. The Order came after a gap of 17 months and the Apex Court has issued environmental guidelines to the government. The SC has ordered the state government to create a national regulator which will grant permission to projects of similar nature and an imposition of heavy fines to polluting industries. Lafarge, on the other hand, has promised to compensate affected people in form of employment and to people affected due to pollution by constructing hospitals and schools for them.

Oil and Petroleum Exploration and Drilling in Manipur

The western margin of Manipur constitutes a portion of basinal (geosynclinal) part of the Assam-Arakan Oil Basin. This has been categorized by the Ministry of Petroleum and Natural Gas, Government of India as belonging to Category-I Basin (proven petroliferous basin). Sediments of over 10 km thick and ranging in age from Upper Cretaceous to Recent is present in the fold and thrust belt (Naga Schuppen Belt). Eocene-Pliocene sequence contains potential source, reservoir and cap rock. More than 40 oil and gas fields have been discovered from the nearby basin.[28]

One of the development processes which has flouted all human rights norms on indigenous peoples' rights in Manipur is the case of provision of licensing for oil exploration and drilling in Manipur by the Government of India to a Multinational Company without informing and taking the consent of the indigenous peoples.[29] The Ministry of Petroleum and Natural Gas, Government of India granted licence to Jubiliant Oil and Gas Private Limited, based in Noida, a Multinational Oil Company in 2009, the headquarters of which is based in the Netherlands, for exploration and drilling works.[30]

Under the Eighth round of New Exploration Licensing Policy (NELP-VIII), the Government of India have signed one production sharing contract on 19th July, 2010 at New Delhi for onland oil block in Manipur, codenamed (AA-ONN-2009/1) with the Jubilant Oil & Gas Pvt. Limited.[31] The total area granted for oil exploration is 3850 square kilometres, which is almost one sixth of total geographical area of Manipur. The Government without informing the people had already undertaken extensive surveys for oil exploration in Tamenglong, Jiribam and Churachandpur Districts, where the Zeliangrong, Meitei, Hmar and Kuki peoples reside.

Further, signing of the agreement, memorandum of understanding and other procedure, which are done normally for such task, have been executed stealthily between the

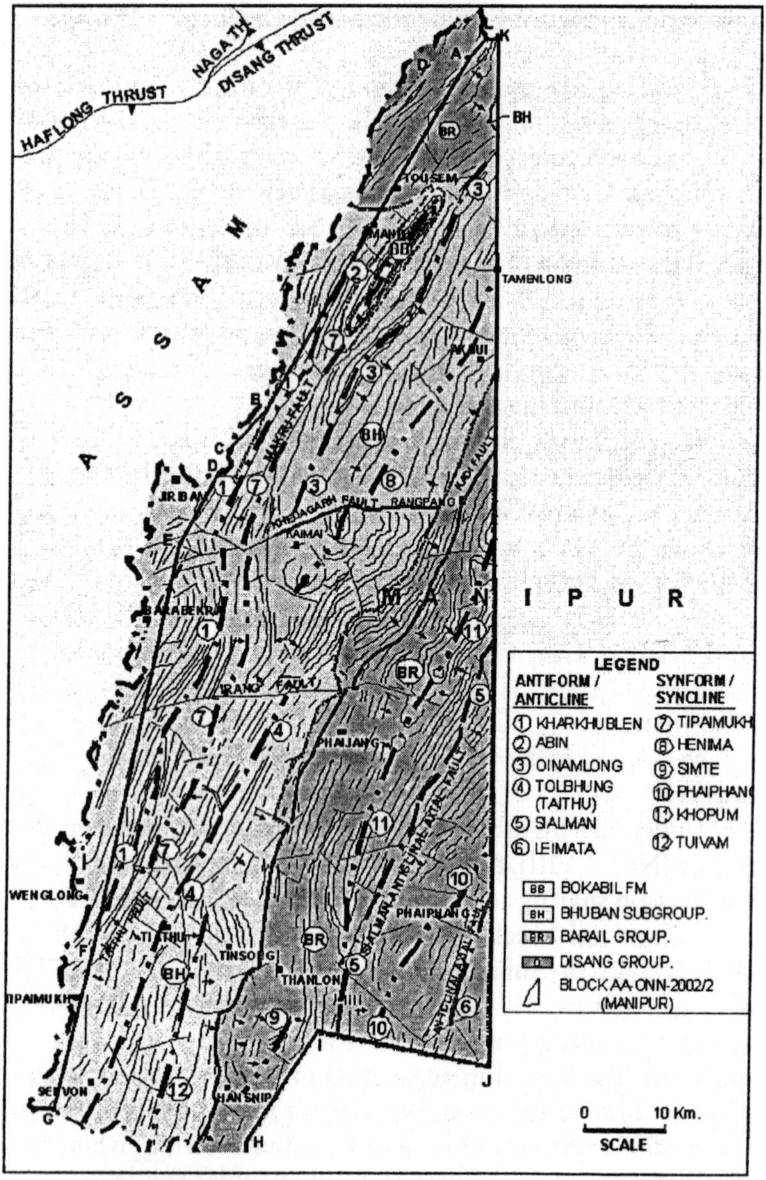

Source: Reliant Energy.

Fig. 4.1: Map showing the Petroleum Deposits in Manipur

Government and implementing agency (company) and hence did not take prior fair and informed consent of the people thereby violating the Article 10 of the United Nations Declaration on the Rights of Indigenous Peoples.

In the years 2003 and 2009, the Government had undertaken a comprehensive promotional exercise to promote the oil blocks through road-shows at New Delhi, London, Houston, Calgary and Perth, inviting bids for Oil Corporate bodies for explorations. These licensing is in the premise setting that all hydrocarbon deposits in India belongs to the Union[32], which completely contradicts the provisions of United Nations Declaration on the Rights of Indigenous Peoples which mentions clearly that all resources in indigenous peoples land belongs to them and they have exclusive rights own, control and mange their own resources in accordance to their wishes and aspirations.

At the moment, the Government of Manipur is facilitating the Alpha Geo Private Limited, based in Hyderabad, India in preparation to conduct Seismic studies at Tamenglong District for necessary explorations.[33] Entry 53 of List I of the Seventh Schedule to the Constitution of India outlined that regulations and development of oilfields and mineral oil resources, petroleum and petroleum products, other liquids and substances declared by Parliament by law to be dangerously inflammable falls under Union list which is in the exclusive control and management of the Central Government of India.

Notwithstanding the absence of free prior and informed consent, there has been no environmental impact assessment due to exploration and drilling in Manipur. Neither there has been any assessment of the impact due to influx of immigrants as oil exploration related exploration and drilling works and increase militarization, which would further aggravate human rights violations, including violence against women.

No one in Manipur is aware of what kind of terms and conditions are laid down in the licensing between the Government and the Jubiliant Oil and Gas private Limited and how the people of Manipur would benefit from this entire process of oil exploration. With the high prevalence of corruption and state priority to maintaining security machinery, the limited loyalty, if provided to Manipur will never reach its peoples, but would rather facilitate more conflict and human rights violations and to more poverty as the territory and resource which they depend for survival are taken away and polluted. There is no information as to how the oil will be transported and whether new pipelines would be laid and whether these pipelines would be an additional source of environmental catastrophe and rights violations.

The efforts to explore and drill oil in Manipur involves a process of disrespect and non-application of human rights based approach to development, one that recognizes indigenous peoples rights, more with self-determined development over their land and resources and which integrates universally accepted human rights norms and principles.

The Memorandum placed the following demands[34]:

1. The plan for the exploration of petroleum is in the territory of the indigenous people where Government of India and the company fail to seek the free, fair and prior informed consent of the indigenous people under the ILO Convention 107 and UN Declaration on the Rights of the Indigenous People. It is mandatory to ask the Government of India to seek the free, fair and prior inform consent of the people without any delay;
2. No systematic Environmental Impact Assessment (EIA) has been done and it should be requested to do before starting the exploration works;
3. There is no plan for relocation of the indigenous people who are going to be displaced from their traditional land. Thus, rehabilitation and resettlement should be done before commencing the exploration work. It is

worth to mention here that Rehabilitation and Resettlement (R&R) for the displaced people due to any kind of developmental project is mandatory, however, no R&R has been done properly for those projects which are already completed; and

4. Sharing of the earning from the petroleum with the people of Manipur is not clear. We demand equitable share from it.

Box 4.1: Crude Oil Seepage hits Naga Villages, PIL filed

The Gauhati High Court has directed motion counsels representing two oil-spill affected villages in Nagaland, to issue notices to the Oil and Natural Gas Corporation Ltd. (ONGC) and a number of departments of the Government of India and Nagaland. Court held a hearing for admission of the Public Interest Litigation (PIL) today, Monday, September 12, filed against the Oil and Natural Gas Corporation Ltd., the Basin Manager of ONGC, Cinnamara in Jorhat, Ministry of Environment and Forests, Government of India, the State of Nagaland, the Nagaland Geology and Mining Department, Nagaland Forest Department, the Nagaland State Pollution Control Board and the Union of India represented by the Ministry of Petroleum and another, the Natural Gas and the Ministry of Environment and Forests, Government of India.

The PIL was filed by Mhonlumo Kikon and others, representing Changpang village and Tssori village in Wokha district of Nagaland against the crude oil giant and the governments. In the PIL the two villages – Nagaland's only two areas rich in crude petroleum – have sought at least Rs. 1,000 crore as consolidated compensation to the villagers for environmental, agricultural and economic damage allegedly caused by the about 16 years of unabated oil spillage from the ONGC's abandoned oil rigs.

Sources informed tonight that the High Court heard the PIL and directed the counsels of the petitioners to issue notices to the stated respondents. Picking up the case, sources informed that the High Court would be holding the next hearing somewhere in the first week of November this year.

The matter was heard in the Court of the Chief Justice and Justice Meruno in the Guwahati High Court, the sources said. As reported earlier in The Morung Express, the demands stated in the PIL are several. For instance, the petitioners are seeking Rs. 1,000 crore compensation for the affected villagers, criminal proceedings against ONGC and government officials and departments, clearing the affected area of spilt oil; Court order against any negotiation, understanding or permission with the ONGC or other companies (Indian and foreign) working on oil exploration, extraction or production to explore, extract oil in the state of Nagaland till the issue of oil spill affected area is redressed.

Source: North East People Alliance, September 13, 2011.

Box 4.2: Online Petition "Save Changpang and Tsorri Villages from ONGC Oil Spills in Nagaland"

Oil spills from Oil and Natural Gas Corporation (ONGC) well sites in Wokha district of Nagaland, India have severely destroyed Changpang and Tsorri villages of the district. More than two thousand indigenous Lotha Naga peoples of the villages have seen the farmlands, forests and water sources they rely on for their survival contaminated due to the spillage, including their spiritual sites. Further, health problems in the district have increased significantly in this area since the spillage, with higher rates of water-borne diseases, malnutrition, miscarriages, cancer, kidney failure and nerve problems.

The ONGC began extraction since 1981 after acquiring permission from the Government of Nagaland in 1973 to explore oil and natural gas in the villages without obtaining the Free Prior and Informed Consent of the indigenous communities as per the national and international law [Art. 371(A) of the Constitution of India and UNDRIP Art. 19]. As per the provisions of Art. 371(A), both mineral and surface resources belong to the communities and not the State. Only after continued protests by numerous civil society groups for over a decade, the government withdrew permission in 1994.

Due to improper and careless capping of the oil well sites, oil spillage has continued for over 17 years now and continues to affect the lives of the peoples in the villages. Before the extraction was stopped, the ONGC is estimated to have produced more than 1.2 million metric tons of oil from this area yet the company appears not to have used a portion of the profit from this for making sure the sites were properly secured.

Recently, a case has been filed at Guwahati High Court against the ONGC, Government of Nagaland and its affiliated departments that is going on. We need your urgent support to save the villages and attain justice for harms the villagers suffered.

Source: North-east People Alliance, February 22, 2012.

Conclusion

Investment is needed uplifting the economy of the state. As far as mining and oil exploration and extraction are concerned Union laws can easily bypass state legislations. As we have seen in the case of Odisha and Meghalaya, the Union laws override state legislation. The case of Meghalaya is merits attention. Mining at low scale has been a traditional practice of the indigenous people in the state, which state legislations recognize. At the same time, customary laws related with landownership and lease is a legislated piece of legal safeguard in the state unlike Manipur. In spite of the existence of such laws, Lafarge could come out victorious. Compared to

Manipur and Odisha, Manipur is at a fragile state, both in terms of absence of laws as well as given the votility of the social composition of population. As of now, conflict originating from mineral resources has not taken place in Manipur. On the brighter side, communities, irrespective of tribe and ethnic affiliations came out together to oppose the move against oil exploration and drilling by Reliant Energy. However, the proposed Inida-EU FTA is likely to exacerbate displacement and dispossession of the peoples' right to own resources and conserve them. The FTA is likely to weaken the existing legislative safeguards such as laws related with lease, rental and ownership. It would also entail influx of skilled non-local labourers and deny work opportunities to the natives.

Finally, information related with ores and metals are closely guarded, given the tag of national wealth. What puts Manipur at stake is that apart from information partially made public, there can be no access to information on the availability of ores, minerals and metals. Thus, other than, these public materials, others, such as availability of uranium, and plans for investment from willing parties, are kept as confidential. Given the closely guarded nature of the negotiations related with the proposed India-EU FTA, one is not sure if already plans are afoot for investment in these sectors. Thus, the civil society bodies region working in the areas of livelihood and human security have every reason to be apprehensive about the three-day maiden visit in May 2012 by a delegation of ambassadors from European countries to Nagaland.

Notes

1. *The Telegraph*, Kolkota, May 15, 2012.
2. www.sinlung.com/2012/02/us-keen-to-invest-in-northeast-india.html#ixzz26yXDptvN
3. *Draft Industrial and Investment Policy of Manipur, 2011.*
4. *Ibid.*
5. *Ibid.*

6. "Chromite exploration in Manipur", *Seven Sisters Post*, Kolkota, May 10, 2012.
7. Sobhapati Samom, "Chromite mining project opposed by Manipur bodies", *The Assam Tribune*, Guwahati, Wednesday, October 22, 2008.
8. *Ibid.*
9. *Ibid.*
10. *Ibid.*
11. *Ibid.*
12. *Ibid.*
13. *Ibid.*
14. *Ibid.*
15. AIR, 1961 (2) SCR 536.
16. AIR, 1961 (2) SCR 537.
17. AIR 1970 SC 1436.
18. *Ibid.*
19. *Ibid.*
20. Forum for Indigenous Perspectives and Action, *The Negation of Indigenous Peoples Territory: The Case of Lafarge Cement in Meghalaya, NE India*, Imphal, 2007.
21. *Ibid.*
22. *Ibid.*
23. *Ibid.*
24. "Lafarge can't do limestone mining in Meghalaya: SC", *Economic Times*, February 8, 2010.
25. *Ibid.*
26. *Ibid.*
27. http://www.lawisgreek.com/sc-court-allows-lafarge-cement-continue-mining-meghalaya-after-17-months
28. NELP VIII.
29. Memorandum submitted to The Special Representative, The Secretary General on the Issues of Human Rights and Transnational Corporations and Other Business Enterprises, United Nation's Organisation, Geneva by North east Dialogue Forum, Imphal on November 29, 2011.
30. Signing of PSC for AA-ONN-2009/2 Under NELP-VIII, *Source:* http://www.dghindia.org/nelpviiiblock.aspx
31. "Manipuri gi Block ani dagi Petroleum Louthoknaba 'Jubiliant Energy' da exploration licence Pikhre", the *Poknapham Daily*, Imphal, April 25, 2011.
32. The Oil Fields (Regulation and Development) Act 1948, *The Oil Industry (Development) Act 1974*; Petroleum and Minerals Pipelines (Acquisition of Right of User in Land), Act 1962; and Petroleum and Natural Gas Rules, 1959, Industries (Development and Regulation) Act 1951.

33. Circular of the Director, Commerce and Industry Department, Government of Manipur, Date 31 March, 2011, Memo no. D(5)-15(1)/IND/2010/IH7; "Manipuri gi Block ani dagi Petroleum Louthoknaba 'Jubiliant Energy' da exploration licence Pikhre", the *Poknapham Daily*, Imphal, April 25, 2011.
34. *Op. cit.*, Memorandum, November 29, 2011.

5

Food Security and Livelihood Options in an EU-India Free Trade Regime

The ongoing EU-India Free Trade Agreement includes a number of provisions relating to agriculture and its allied activities. The main concern in the Indian scenario has been the exposure of agriculture to the forces of free trade which will pave way for vulnerability of food security and livelihood as agriculture account for maximum number of workforce in the country. The major apprehension is that the Free Trade Agreement (FTA) will make India dependent on international trade for basic food security. Moreover, entry of firms in India will divert agriculture resources to cash cropping through contract farming as European interest is in non-food grain agro-business such as wines, beers, spirit etc. Whether the agriculture sector is in the list of items for the FTA or not, operationalization EU-India FTA will generate a series of reaction or negative trickledown effects which is going to severely affect the food security and the livelihood options, the area that is the concern for most of the people cutting across every section. The structural changes brought by the implementation of EU-India FTA will definitely impact these two areas. Food security and livelihoods are two most vulnerable areas of an economy when expose to external agents. The process of liberalization carried out in the early

1990s has sown the negative impacts on the economy of Manipur. The issue of food security in the state is very crucial from the point that the state has limited agricultural land and its size is depleting day-by-day owing to haphazard urbanization process of the state. The present chapter will look to the likely effects of the proposed agreement on the food security and livelihood patterns of the state.

Brief Background to Food Security in Manipur

The issue of food security has grown momentum and has become serious issue and challenge in the global community owing to the emerging widespread prevalence of poverty mostly in developing countries. Food and Agriculture Organization (FAO) defines food security as a situation in which "all people, at all times, have physical and economic access to sufficient, safe and nutritious food to meet their dietary needs and food preferences for an active and healthy life." So, the notion of food security has four basic components: availability, accessibility, utilization and stabilization. The four components of food security, viz. availability is a function of production, accessibility is related to purchasing power, utilization is determined by the availability of minimum basic needs, i.e. safe drinking water, primary health care, primary education, proper housing facilities, environmental hygiene and fourth one, stabilization is influenced by the extent of attention given to the sustainability of the system. Though all the aspects of food security is crucial for any region, but the primary aspects, i.e. availability is the cause of concern for Manipur. The study will look into primarily the aspects of availability which is a function of production as the deficit of food grains is increasing at a alarming rate and will be more grim when the proposed Free Trade Agreement (FTA) is set in motion. Though self-sufficiency in food grains is not a sufficient condition for food security, it is taken a primary concern as other aspects will be built on the self-sufficiency. Moreover, the problem is not more of distributive factor but rather low production which always felt short of requirement and had to be adjusted through Public Distribution System (PDS) and import from other states and even from Myanmar. The study will focus on rice as it is the staple food crop and more than 90 per cent of the total cultivated area is under rice.

Food Security: Historical Roots and Beyond

Manipur has a rich history of surplus food grains and its self-reliant capacity has depleted in the recent times. The art of crop husbandry especially rice in the state date back to early period of A.D. The people of the Manipur have rich history of harnessing its water resources for agriculture purposes. The art of dredging rivers and digging new courses were master in the first century A.D. and the peasantry had become a solid aspect of life. The two river systems of Imphal River and Iril River were regularly dredged for communication and transport as well as for irrigation. Later on the temporary damming of rivers and supplying of water to the fields through canal were carried out in the fifth century A.D. This is known as the *Thigel* (damming) and *Ithai* (diversion of water) *Loukhong Complex*. The complex which were built on community labour, still exist.[1] With this rich art of water management system, wet paddy cultivation—broadcasting as well as transplanting was practiced. In the northern and eastern hills of the state, terracing rather than jhum cultivation had led to settled tribal life.[2] British agents and writers like Brown[3] and Pemberton[4] had reported very high yield and productivity owing to its specialized crop husbandry in the state. Brown reported average yield of 4050 kg per *paree*. If converted to modern day measurement, it accounts to 3375 kg per hectare which is hard to attain in the post-green revolution. Brown also estimated that one year produce was enough to feed the population for two years. Not only high production or productivity, the whole administration and socio-political matrix of the Native Rule revolved round rice economy and cultivating land of rice. Land cultivation, measurement and collection of land rent formed an important administrative part of king during the Native Rule. Land administration was important for revenue generation and also for a self-sufficient agrarian economy.

British colonialism was built on this strong and vibrant rice economy. Rice economy was the nucleus of the British colonial economy. Rice was an important source of revenue for the colonial ruler and formed the most important export item resulting from huge surplus extraction. Table 5.1 shows the amount of rice exported during the colonial period (1900-01 to 1938-39). In the year 1900-01, 2655 tonnes of rice was exported from Manipur and it increased almost five fold and reached 14143 in 1938-39.

Table 5.1: Export of Rice from Manipur (1900-01 to 1938-39)

Year	*Rice (tonnes)*
1900-01	2655
1911-12	4107
1924-25	7589
1932-33	10541
1934-35	9334
1938-39	14143

Source: Various Administrative Reports.

Colonial Economy, Artificial Scarcity of Rice and the Nupi Lan in Manipur

The extremity of colonial extraction from rice economy was evident from the *Nupi Lan* (women's war against the export of rice) of 1939. Historically, the *Nupi Lan* had its immediate cause in the artificial famine of 1939 caused by the profiteering activities of the Mayang (Indian) traders who exported rice to colonial garrisons outside Manipur. In another sense, *Nupi Lan* had its immediate cause in an artificial famine of rice due to profiteering activities of speculators drifting the people to ruin and famine. When the ban hitherto enforced on the export of rice was lifted in 1939 to the great advantage of the Mayangs, the price of paddy soared up, thus, seriously affecting the local petty traders, mostly women, and the poor consumers as well. The atmosphere of agitation was looming with the women traders ready to take a course of action against the inflation and the starving stomachs.

In November 1939 when the harvesting was in full swing, the ban hitherto enforce in the export of rice was suddenly lifted, with the result that the mill-owners started heavy buying of the new paddy with the object storming it up and making large profits afterwards. The price of paddy soared up; the numerous petty traders and poorhouse holders were thus deprived of their supplies of paddy; so that in midst of plenty there was starvation. On 12th December, 1939, hundreds of women who were demanding an end to the free trade on rice[5] besieged the president of the Manipur State Durbar[6] and the officials who came to the rescue of the president.[7] In the scuffle that broke out[8] between the women and the Assam Rifles[9], twenty-one women and one Indian officer and seven other ranks of the Assam Rifles were injured.[10] In the following months, women targeted the rice-mills owned by the Mayangs[11], which, "with a daily outturn of 11,200 mounds of rice, absorb the entire paddy available in the state (and)... threw out of employment the bulk of the people who lived by husking." Women boycotted the main bazar, i.e. the hub of hoarding and profiteering that was under colonial protection and protest meetings were held in the Police Bazar.[12] They formed vanguards, intercepted rice carters carrying paddy for sale to the Mayang and at times threw cartloads of rice into gutter.[13] In January 1940 alone they held up about 150 rice loaded carts. In the course of the months long struggle women besieged state thana and fought several pitch battles with the security personnel.[14] In one of the pitch battles fought on 14 January, forty women agitators and some men were injured.[15] Women organized anti-tax gathering and the leaders advised the agitators to arm themselves with tem (a long wooden appliance used for weaving cloth) and wear two phaneks (sarong type of cloth worn by the women of Manipur) while confronting tax-collectors.[16] In short, there was a qualitative shift of the movement towards popular struggle for a responsible government. The movement, however, subsided as a result of the approach of the Second World War in Manipur in early 1940s.

Nupi Lan has to be seen against the background of the rise of Mayang power in Manipur. By 1939 the Mayangs, being the protected British Subject in Manipur, were able to establish as monopoly rights holders in cotton trade, vehicular traffic[17], tea-seed trade, silk manufacturing right, growing mulberry or silk farming[18] right to fell and log some of the trees on the borders of the Kabow Valley[19], bees-wax and agar[20], elephant tusk, deer horn and orchids[21], Rubber Mahal[22], jade[23] and Chalmugra Seed Mahal[24], Orchid Mahal and so on. Mayang control of the economy under British rule and their economic oppression of the people was revealed in an application addressed to the judicial members, Manipur State Durbar dated, 28th September, 1920:

> [That] your humble petitioners are extremely aggrieved at the hard lot of the carters or cart owners who owe money to the Marwari mahajans. They are compelled to carry the goods of their mahajans at a lower rate of annas 8 or 12 or even Re 1 per maund than the ordinary market rate of hire, as they are not allowed to look to any means for their gains.... Moreover, according to the system of compound interest and to carry a few maunds in excess in every cart gratis. Moreover, there are the occasional insertions of fake and real accounts against their name in the *khata* for taking some necessaries of the cart. They even take interest on the value of the articles after turning them into capital. Thus, after the end of the year when all accounts are settled and

> the interests are changed into capital, is spite of their hard labour throughout the year to clear the debt by occasional payment of the little savings of the wages they find to their great astonishment that about the same of even greater capital than that of the last year. Then they are compelled to write another bond in the *khata* for the coming year. Thus...they...gradually increases year by year till it is beyond their power of clearing it.

Under the forced 'liberal trade' and forced taxation of the people there was underdevelopment of Manipur, which was marked by a decline of local production and increase both in the quantity and volume of import, which had a corresponding adverse impact in the balance of payment.[25] Colonial economy was largely responsible for an objective material condition of 'underdevelopment' characterised by decline of Manipur's economy from 'self-sufficiency' into an economy that fully depended on imports from other regions. It subverted interests of various sections of the peoples[26] in varying ways. In other words there was collective subordination of the people and their national aspiration.

Food Security in the Post-British Period

The revivification of rice surplus state after the Second World War was discommoding. The post-British witnessed a complete turnaround in the agrarian economy of the state. The state was reduced from a net exporter of rice during the colonial period to a net importer after the merger with Indian Union, though some small/negligible amount of rice was exported during the pre-statehood period. Table 5.2 shows amount of rice exported from Manipur from 1967 onwards.

From 1967 to 1970 the state exported 7284.30 tonnes of rice. And in 1972 and 1985 the state exported negligible amount of rice, i.e. 40.7 and 10.6 tonnes respectively. The state becomes heavily dependent on the import of rice from

Table 5.2: Export of Rice from Manipur (1967 to 2006)

Year	*Rice (tonnes)*
1967	45.3
1968	6101
1969	930
1970	208
1971	0
1972	40.7
1973-1984	0
1985	10.6
1986-2006	0

Source: Export-Import Files, Marketing Intelligence Department, Government of Manipur.

outside the state. Forces and counter forces came into interplay in shaping the state a very dependent in terms of food grains. On the one hand both production and productivity increases after the Green Revolution, on the other hand population increases on a very rapid scale, the state remains dependent on the import of food grain from outside. In other words, the increase of productivity with the application of HYVs, irrigations, chemical fertilizers (the state has high consumption rate of fertilizer, 105 kg/ha than North East average 78 kg/ha and all India average, 90 kg/ha) in the post-Green Revolution gave an inducement to rice production in the state. But it cannot feed the burgeoning population of the state. As the state has limited cultivable area due to hostile topography, the increase of production and productivity was the result of new technology. Table 5.3 shows the area, production and yield of rice in Manipur from 1960 to 2008.

The productivity growth in terms of yield of rice have been impressive in Manipur as compared to India. The productivity trend shows that rice productivity of Manipur was low up to early 90s and but more than Indian average. From the mid-90s its productivity has touched 2300 mark and is consistently maintaining the trend. In 2008-09 the percentage of difference for the yield rate between India and Manipur is 8.22.

Table 5.3: Area, Production and Yield of Rice in Manipur, 1960 to 2008

Year	Area (000 ha)	Production (000 tn)	Yield (Kg/ha)
1960	162.20	127.00	782.98
1961	161.50	107.00	662.54
1962	161.80	108.00	667.49
1963	160.50	109.00	679.13
1964	160.50	185.00	1152.7
1965	160.50	218.70	1362.6
1966	160.90	260.00	1615.9
1967	174.00	246.00	1413.8
1968	167.00	300.00	1796.4
1969	144.00	232.00	1611.1
1970	140.00	184.20	1315.7
1971	136.00	158.56	1165.9
1972	146.60	152.16	1037.9
1973	169.78	238.62	1405.5
1974	176.51	274.68	1556.2
1975	177.19	276.42	1560.0
1976	177.20	266.97	1506.6
1977	179.13	299.98	1674.7
1978	159.56	255.21	1599.5
1979	155.20	227.53	1466.0
1980	188.55	273.04	1448.1
1983	161.22	255.13	1582.5
1984	167.41	332.99	1989.1
1985	164.60	332.53	2020.2
1986	165.14	242.47	1467.3
1987	165.76	312.76	1886.8
1988	167.06	319.72	1913.8
1989	162.37	245.12	1509.6
1990	157.41	274.17	1741.8
1991	160.30	340.45	2123.8
1992	151.19	273.12	1806.5
1993	161.87	348.82	2154.9
1994	163.93	358.51	2187.0
1995	134.93	338.05	2505.4
1996	166.10	367.28	2211.2
1997	157.90	351.67	2227.2
1998	166.89	382.19	2290.1
1999	157.05	364.98	2324.0
2000	156.96	381.69	2431.8
2001	162.57	387.26	2382.11
2002	153.11	335.67	2192.35
2003	157.83	381.24	2415.51
2004	176.31	435.93	2472.52
2005	166.23	386.07	2322.09
2006	165.37	389.17	2353.33
2007	166.15	406.15	2444.48
2008	168.40	396.96	2357.20

Sources: 1. Government of India, Estimates of Area and Production of Principal Crops in India, Various issues.

2. Government of Manipur, Directorate of Economics and Statistics, *Statistical Handbook of Manipur* 2002, p. 77 and *Statistical Abstract of Manipur* 1998, p. 91, Statistical Abstract of Manipur 1998—Various Economic Surveys.

Table 5.4: Comparative Rice Yield in (kg/ha) of Manipur and India

Year	*Manipur*	*India*
1960-61	783	1013
1970-71	1316	1123
1980-81	1450	1336
1990-91	1742	1740
1995-96	2505	1797
1996-97	2211	1882
1997-98	2227	1900
1998-99	2290	1921
1999-00	2324	1986
2000-01	2431	1961
2001-02	2382	2078
2002-03	2192	1804
2003-04	2416	2078
2004-05	2473	1984
2005-06	2322	2102
2006-07	2353	2131
2007-08	2444	2202
2008-09	2357	2178

Source: Same as Table 5.3.

Table 5.5: Compound growth Rates of Area, Production and Yield of Rice

(In per cent per annum)

Period	*Area*	*Production*	*Yield*
1960-1970	0.28	12.57	12.88
1970-1980	1.95	5.59	3.57
1980-1990	0.68	1.39	2.08
1990-2000	0.15	2.75	2.59
2000-2008	0.88	0.49	–0.39
1960-2008	0.08	2.40	2.32

Source: Calculated from Table 5.3.

The compound growth rate of area in the state declines from 0.28 in 1960-61-1969-70 to 0.15 in 1990-91-2000-01. In the early phase of Green Revolution both growth rate of production and yield touch 12 per cent mark, i.e. for production 12.57 and yield 12.88 in 1960-1970 but it also starts declining. But looking at the overall from 1960-2008 production and productivity almost matches, i.e. 2.36 and 2.38, depicting positive impact of Green Revolution. But the area under rice cultivation remain almost same, it depicts that neither net nor gross sown area increase.

But the state was not comfortable in keeping the state a self-sufficient in food grains due to inflated population particularly with the influx of migrants. The state experienced a high percentage decennial growth rate. The annual growth in area sown for the period 1982-1992 was 1.43 per cent. During the decade 1991-2001, the net area sown had, in fact, declined whereas the population had grown at an annual rate of 3 per cent. As a result of this asymmetric growth in area sown and population, which leads to stagnant yield, the state is facing an increasing deficit in rice production.[27] Table 5.6 shows population growth in terms of hill-valley and percentage share of rural and urban population.

Table 5.6: Population Growth in Manipur (1951 Census to 2011 Census)

Year	*Persons*	*Percentage Annual Growth*	*Percentage Decennial Growth*			*Percentage of Urban Population*	*Percentage of Rural Population*
			Manipur	*Hills*	*Valley*		
1951	577635	—	—	—	—	0.05	99.05
1961	780037	3.00	35.04	—	—	8.68	91.32
1971	1072753	3.19	37.53	—	—	13.19	86.81
1981	1420953	2.81	32.46	41.27	28.22	26.42	73.58
1991	1837149	2.57	29.29	32.38	27.65	27.52	72.48
2001	2293896	2.22	24.86	35.46	19.04	25.01	74.09
2011	2721756	1.72	18.65	NA	NA	NA	NA

Source: Government of Manipur (2008), *Statistical Abstract Manipur 2007*, Directorate of Economics and Statistics; Census of India 2011, Provisional Report.

The state registered a very high decennial growth of 35.04, 37.53, and 32.46 in 1961, 1971 and 1981 respectively and it declines to 24.86 per cent in 2001. The high percentage growth in 1961 and 1971 was the result of influx of migrants. Percentage annual growth rate hover around 2 and half. The hill registered high growth rate than the valley. Majority of the population are inhibited in the rural areas, almost 75 per cent of the total population live in the rural area. The increasing population is felt on the food demand. Table 5.7 shows the production, requirements and shortage of rice in Manipur from 1972 to 2006.

Table 5.7: Production, Requirements and Shortage of Rice in Manipur (1972 to 2006)

('000 tonnes)

Year	*Requirement of Rice*	*Production of Rice*	*Shortage of Rice*	*Percentage Shortage & Surplus*
1972	232.59	152.16	–80.43	–34.58
1973	239.9	238.62	–1.28	–0.53
1974	247.21	274.68	27.47	11.11
1975	254.85	279.42	24.57	9.64
1976	261.85	266.97	5.12	1.96
1977	269.15	299.98	30.83	11.45
1978	276.46	255.02	–21.26	–7.69
1979	283.78	227.53	–56.25	–19.82
1980	291.09	273.04	–18.05	–6.20
1981	298.4	253.14	–45.26	–15.17
1982	305.71	219.47	–86.24	–28.20
1983	313.02	255.18	–57.84	–18.48
1984	320.34	232.99	–87.35	–27.27
1985	327.65	332.53	4.88	1.49
1986	334.96	242.47	–92.49	–27.61
1987	342.27	358.64	16.37	4.78
1988	363.66	326.82	–36.84	–10.13
1989	367.89	245.12	–122.77	–33.40
1990	386.81	274.00	–112.87	–29.18
1991	360.63	340.45	–20.18	–5.60
1992	368.89	273.12	–95.77	–25.96
1993	377.56	348.82	–28.74	–7.61
1994	386.29	358.51	–27.78	–7.19
1995	395.09	338.05	–57.04	–14.44
1996	403.95	367.28	–36.67	–9.08
1997	412.87	351.67	–61.02	–14.82
1998	421.83	382.19	–39.64	–9.40
1999	430.83	364.98	–65.85	–15.28
2000	439.88	381.73	–58.15	–13.22
2001	449.37	387.26	–62.11	–13.82
2002	458.53	335.67	–122.86	–26.79
2003	468.02	381.24	–86.78	–18.54
2004	477.56	435.93	–41.63	–8.72
2005	487.16	386.07	–101.09	–20.75
2006	496.82	389.17	–107.65	–21.67

Source: Various Statistical Handbooks and Abstract of Manipur, Directorate of Economics and Statistics, Government of Manipur.

The state fell short of the requirement except for the year 1974-77, 1985 and 1987. In these six years the state manages to generate rice surplus of 27.47, 24.57, 5.12, 30.83, 4.88 and 16.37 tonnes respectively. Looking at the trend, requirement is creeping up all the time and the production is not able to catch up the requirements resulting in huge shortages. In 2005 and 2006 the shortage of rice was a massive 101 and 107 thousand tonnes respectively, i.e. a percentage shortage of 20.75 in 2005 and 21.67 in 2006 and the trend will not easily reverse.

In the post-Green Revolution phase, both the productivity (rice yield per hectare in the state, 2273 kg is higher than both the North East Region, 1567 kg and all India average, 1913 kg) and production increase but the state never reach the comfort zone of self-sufficient in food grains. The factors are numerous but some worth mentioning are lack of and proper utilization of irrigation, lack of institutional credit, marginalization of landholdings, demographic pressure, lethargic approach from the Government, pathetic scene of rice cultivation in hills etc. Even the Draft Annual Plan 2007-08, for agriculture has identified lack of adequate and reliable irrigation infrastructure, lack of adequate infrastructure for mobilizing development programme in the hills as major constraints during the Tenth Five Year Plan 2002-07 to the production of food grains. The contour of the evolving agrarian economy in the state is explained by the existing agrarian structure and relation.

Landholding Pattern

Landholding is an important parameter in agriculture for explaining the nature, status, strength of agrarian economy. Marginalization of landholding is the present trend in the state and is severely affecting the agarian economy. Marginalization is predominantly the result of high population pressure especially in the rural areas (see Table 5.8). According to the

2001 Census, 74 per cent population lives in the rural area. Both the NSS and Census data show marginalization of operational landholding in the state.

Table 5.8: Distribution of Operational Holdings in Rural Areas of Manipur (NSS)

Size Class	*1991-92*			*2002-03*		
	No. of hhs (00)	*Area (00 hect)*	*Average area*	*No. of hhs (00)*	*Area (00 hect)*	*Average Area*
Marginal (Less than 1 hectare)	1204 (71.12)	489 (37.44)	0.41	1918 (82.57)	844 (59.65)	0.44
Small (1 to 2 hectares)	340 (20.08)	459 (35.15)	1.35	355 (15.28)	441 (31.16)	1.24
Semi-Medium (2 to 4 hectares)	148 (8.74)	355 (27.18)	2.40	45 (1.94)	104 (7.35)	2.31
Medium (4 to 10 hectares)	1 (0.06)	3 (0.23)	3.00*	5 (0.21)	26 (1.84)	5.2
Large (10 hectares & above)	—	—	—	—	—	—
All Holdings	**1693 (100)**	**1306 (100)**	**0.77**	**2323 (100)**	**1415 (100)**	**0.61**

Note: Figures in the parentheses indicate the percentage distribution.

Sources: 1. NSSO, 1997. Operational Landholdings in India 1991-92: Salient Features, 48th Round, Report No. 407.

2. NSSO, 2006. Some Aspects of Operational Landholdings in India 2002-03, 59th Round, Report No. 491.

Operational holdings in rural Manipur as given by NSS is shown in Table 5.8. From 1992 to 2002 the number of operational holdings has increased by 63 thousand and area by 11 thousand resulting in the decrease of average size of operational holding from 0.77 hectare to 0.61 hectare. For marginal holdings, number of households increased by 59 per cent and area by 72 per cent. The momentum increased in marginal holdings mainly comes from the breakdown of semi-medium holders where both the number of households and area operated declined by about 70 per cent. In the case of small holdings while the number of households increased by

4.4 per cent the area operated has reduced by 2.2 per cent and for semi-medium holdings. Contrarily there is an increase in both number of households and area operated under medium holdings.

Table 5.9 shows distribution of operational holdings in the state according to 1990-91, 1995-96 and 2000-01 agricultural censuses. As per the Agricultural Census 2000-01 the area of operational holding is about 172 thousand hectares operated by 149 thousand farmers. The number of marginal holders increases from 69 thousand in 1990-91 to 75 thousand in 2000-01. In 2000-01, the marginal and small holders account for 83 per cent of operational land holders. Large holders are virtually non-existent. The average size of operational holdings for Manipur has slightly decreased from 1.22 hectares in 1995-96 to 1.15 hectares in 2000-01. The area operated in small and marginal holdings accounted for 59.88 per cent in 2000-01. Average size of operational holdings of all holders has also declined— for marginal 0.55 in 1990-91 to 0.53 in 2000-01, for small 1.37 in 1990-91 to 1.29 in 2000-01, for semi-medium 2.57 in 1990-91 to 2.47 in 2000-01, for medium 5.00 in 1990-91 to 4.86 in 2000-01 and for large 12.16 in 1990-91 to 11.38 in 2000-01.

Marginalization and smallness of holdings have made the farmers very hard to maintain a subsistence level and have discouraged the farmers to invest for private capital formation. Rice cultivation has become a part time job for most of the small and marginal farmers and it has become an enduring proposition rather than a commercial proposition. Now-a-days rice cultivation is driven by push factor rather than pull factor as the farmers do not find any incentive; they are cultivating not because it is profitable or make them subsistence but because they do not want their land to remain idle. As marginal and small farmers seldom get institutional credit, they resort to land for their immediate needs and debt servicing through selling out or mortgaging out their land. As a result, the interlocking of credit and land market is rampant

Table 5.9: Distribution of Operational Holdings in Manipur

Size Class	*1990-91*			*1995-96*			*2000-01*		
	No. ('000)	*Area ('000 hect.)*	*Average (Hect.)*	*No. ('000)*	*Area ('000 hect.)*	*Average (Hect.)*	*No. ('000)*	*Area ('000 hect.)*	*Average (Hect.)*
Marginal	69 (48.59)	38 (21.71)	0.55	69 (48.59)	39 (22.41)	0.57	75 (50.33)	40 (23.25)	0.53
Small	49 (34.50)	67 (38.28)	1.37	49 (34.50)	67 (38.50)	1.37	49 (32.88)	63 (36.63)	1.29
Semi-Medium	21 (14.78)	54 (30.86)	2.57	21 (14.78)	54 (30.85)	2.57	22 (14.77)	55 (31.98)	2.47
Medium	3 (2.11)	15 (8.57)	5	3 (2.11)	14 (8.00)	4.67	3 (2.01)	14 (8.14)	4.86
Large	Neg.	1 (0.57)	12.16	Neg.	Neg	—	Neg	Neg.	11.38
All Size	**142 (100)**	**175 (100)**	**1.23**	**142 (100)**	**174 (100)**	**1.22**	**149 (100)**	**172 (100)**	**1.15**

Note: Figures in the parentheses indicate percentage.
Source: Government of Manipur (2008), Economic Survey Manipur 2007-08, Directorate of Economics and Statistics.

in the rural Manipur. Lands are used not for productive purposes but for consumption purposes through selling or mortgaging out. In some pockets of valley due to lack of inducement in rice cultivation farmers are turning into fishery, their paddy land are converted to fish farms and even selling out for other purposes.

The distribution pattern of landholdings is very much related with the distribution of assets of the cultivating households as the agriculture productivity is dependent upon the types of assets used. The information on inventory assets owned by the cultivating households is available in various rounds of Debt and Investment Survey, NSSO. The distribution of assets per reported cultivating household in 48th and 59th round of NSSO is shown in Table 5.10.

Table 5.10: Distribution of Assets per Reported Cultivating Household in Rupees (48th and 59th Round of NSSO)

Assets	*As on 30.06.1991*		*As on 30.06.2006*	
	Average Value (Rs.)	*Percentage*	*Average Value (Rs.)*	*Percentage*
Land	52776	55.87	121153	60.58
Building	25680	27.18	43442	21.72
Livestock & Poultry	3000	3.18	5523	2.76
Machinery & Equipment	4094	4.33	6543	3.27
Household durables	7516	7.96	13628	6.81
Financial assets	1377	1.46	9671	4.84
Loan receivable	20	0.02	38	0.02
Total	**94463**	**100**	**199998**	**100**

Source: 1. NSSO, 1998. 48th Round, Report No. 419.
2. NSSO, 2006. 59th Round, Report No. 500.

The average value of assets owned by the cultivating household increased from about Rs. 94 thousand in 1991 to Rs. 2 lakh in 2002. Out of all the assets owned by cultivating household, land is still the most important asset. Its share in the average value of the assets owned per reporting household increases from 56 per cent in 1991 to 61 per cent in 2002. The contribution of building to the total asset has declined from 27 to 21 depicting deteriorating living standard of cultivating household. The values of livestock and poultry have also declined from 3.18 to 2.76 portraying weak diversification agricultural allied activities or less incentive. Machinery and equipment also shows a declining trend from 4.33 to 3.27, a clear indication of falling rate of private capital formation among the cultivator. Machines and equipments are owned by affluent cultivators and small and marginal farmers are also deserting bovine for cultivation, service of machine hiring is emerging in rural Manipur. Increase of financial asset may be come from other non-agricultural activities especially trade. Institutional credit is depicted by the small contribution of loan amount. Institutional credit for cultivation is still a far cry for most of the cultivators.

Irrigation Infrastructure

Poor irrigation infrastructure is leading agrarian economy of the state to nowhere. State is still heavily dependent on monsoon for agricultural purpose. Irrigation the most important input of agriculture has received attention only immediately after the attainment of statehood. The first major irrigation project, the Loktak Lift Irrigation (LLI) project was taken up in the year 1973-74 and later in the Fifth Plan besides LLI, new projects comprising three medium river irrigation projects, viz. Imphal Barrage, Sekmai Barrage, Khoupum Dam, and one Multipurpose project—Singda Multipurpose Project, was taken up. By the end of Ninth Plan, the irrigation potential from the completed or partially completed project is 28,500 ha with a utilization of only 20,910 ha. Most of the major and medium irrigation projects are confined to Valley. A number of Minor Irrigation Scheme (MIS), both in the hill and valley has been initiated with a potential of 30,645 ha and utilization capacity of 18,265, i.e. 59.60 per cent.[28] At the end of Tenth Plan the irrigated area is 30,980 ha, i.e. 13.24 per cent of the net agricultural land.[29]

The under utilization as well lack of irrigation has not encouraged double and multiple cropping which would have boost food grain production. Investment in irrigation and drainage not only raised yields directly they also facilitated multiple cropping, thereby raising the year round utilization of both land and labour.[30] Several micro surveys in India comparing agricultural performance in areas commanded by irrigation works and those outside (and in a few cases between irrigated and unirrigated lands in the same area) also show that land is used more intensively (both in terms of the extent of fallowing and of multi-cropping); that irrigated lands grow more of higher productivity, high value crops; and that average yields of practically all crops are substantially higher in irrigated areas. But irrigation system is not producing the desire result in the state. The problem is more of 'maintenance and utilization of assets'. The irrigation facility in the state focuses more on 'creation of assets' and employment generation rather than the 'maintenance, utilization and sustainability of assets'. For rice cultivation, still, the state depends on the timely arrival of monsoon. In other words, the irrigation system in the state cannot reduce, at least to some extent, the overdependence on monsoon. Deformity in irrigation not only discourages double and multiple cropping but also severely affects the use of High Yielding Varieties (HYVs). Looking at the past few years, there is inconsistency in the use of HYVs. Area under HYV and Improved Variety (IV) from 2000 to 2007 is given in Table 5.11.

High Yielding Varieties (HYV)/IV which is predominantly used in the valley shows inconsistency. In 2000-01 and 2001-02, 70.92 and 74.04 thousand hectares in the valley were under HYV/IV. It drastically came down to 38.65 in 2002-03 and 46.42 in 2003-04. Again it increases to 88.62 in 2004-05 and come down again in 2006-07 with 54.10. This affects both the productivity and production. As HYV required timely surveillance of irrigation, with uncertainty in irrigation couple with frequent floods, farmers resort to local variety

Table 5.11: Area under HYV/IV

('000 Hectares)

Year	*Hill*		*Valley*	
	HYV/IV	*Others*	*HYV/IV*	*Others*
2000-01	6.37	61.59	70.92	18.11
2001-02	12.12	59.05	74.04	16.91
2002-03	8.71	64.02	38.65	41.73
2003-04	13.86	63.19	46.42	34.36
2004-05	12.07	62.78	88.62	12.21
2005-06	9.71	72.96	62.39	21.02
2006-07	12.56	67.27	54.01	31.44

Source: Government of Manipur (2008), *Statistical Abstract Manipur* 2007, Directorate of Economics and Statistics.

which can stand untimely irrigation and floods, as a risk management. In the state where agriculture is synonymous with paddy cultivation, the pathetic site of irrigation has not either supercharged the production or increases the net sown area.

Unbalance use of fertilizer and HYV in hill and valley is another cause of concern for the rice economy of the state. HYV and fertilizers are predominantly used in the valley and its used in the hill is marginal. Table 5.12 shows the fertilizer consumption in hill and valley from 2000-01 to 2006-07.

Table 5.12: Region-wise Consumption of Fertilizer in Manipur

(In tonnes)

Year	*Manipur*	*Hill*	*Valley*
2000-01	46747	3006 (6.43)	43741 (93.57)
2001-02	46487	3782 (8.14)	42696 (91.86)
2002-03	56700	4370 (7.71)	52330 (92.29)
2003-04	59046	4957 (8.40)	54089 (91.60)
2004-05	44137	3607 (8.17)	40530 (91.83)
2005-06	30594	2027 (6.63)	28567 (93.37)

Note: Figure in parentheses is percentage to the total.
Source: Government of Manipur (2008), *Statistical Abstract Manipur* 2007, Directorate of Economics and Statistics.

In the last six years the consumption of fertilizers in the hills cannot cross the 10 per cent mark of the state's total consumption. In 2000-01 hill consumes 3006 tonnes of fertilizer, i.e. 6.43 per cent of total consumption which remain almost the same in 2005-06, 2027 (6.63%). Whereas, the valley consumption almost 90 per cent of the state total consumption, i.e. 93.37 per cent in 2005-06. The valley also account for higher percentage use of HYV as compared to hill. The use of high percentage of HYV and fertilizer with better irrigation compare to hill results in higher productivity as well as production of rice. The valley account for 60 per cent of total productivity of rice and hill for 10 per cent in 2006-07 and the yield per hectare of rice is also high as compare to hill. In 2006-07 the yield rate of valley 2742.24 kg/hectare as compares to hill 1907.5 kg/hectare. But the concern is over the high prevalence of jhumming in the hills. The ratio of settled to jhum cultivation in the hills is given in Table 5.13.

Table 5.13: Settled Land *vs.* Jhum Land under Rice in the Hill Districts of Manipur

(In '000 ha)

Year	*Settled*	*Jhum*	*Ratio of Settled to Jhum*
2000-01	28.17	39.79	0.70
2001-02	29.15	42.47	0.68
2002-03	29.55	43.18	0.68
2003-04	35.26	41.79	0.84
2004-05	30.78	44.70	0.68
2005-06	37.07	45.60	0.81
2006-07	45.18	34.65	1.30

Source: Government of Manipur (2008), *Statistical Abstract Manipur* 2007, Directorate of Economics and Statistics.

The ratio of settled to jhum in the hill seems to be improving. In 2000-01 it is 0.70 and it increases to 1.30. This is a positive sign and needs to be sustained. As the agriculture in the state is confined to 10.48 per cent of the total geographical area (the geographical area being 22.327 lakh ha) and the net agricultural area being 2.34 lakh ha[31], there is little scope for expansion of agricultural land in the face of swelling population, urbanization and development process. The situation calls for an urgent policy, practical and physical intervention from the state for restoring the erstwhile food security status. There is very serious concern for the food grains security of the state which is on the verge of exposition to the global juggernaut like EU-India FTA.

Flawed Utilization of Land

A major factor which has a direct bearing on development in general and agro-related activities in Manipur is the pattern of utilization of land. Two existing Acts, and the manner in which they have been employed, have had a negative impact on arable land. The former pertains to Land Acquisition Act, 1894 (extends to the whole of India except the state of Jammu & Kashmir), which has been perpetually (mandatory) used by the State or Central Government to undertake massive development projects for 'public purpose'. The second pertains to Section 20 of the Manipur Land Revenue and Land Reforms Act, 1960, put in place for purpose of revenue collection based on nature of landholding and to avoid diversion of land but hardly given weightage or importance in the case of Manipur. If rightly followed in spirit, this Act can act as a deterrent to increasing instances of converting arable land into settlement areas or other purposes in Manipur.

Section 3(a) of the Land Acquisition Act states, "The expression 'land' include benefits to arise out of land, and things attached to the earth or permanently fastened to anything attached to the earth." The Maharashtra Government amended this section in 1964 stating, "The expression 'arable land' means land fit for cultivation whether in fact cultivated or not; and includes garden land." Sections 4(1) and 4(2) are mandatory to be used by any Government when any land is intended to be acquired by the Government. Section 4(1) reads:

> Whenever, it appears to the [appropriate Government] that land in any locality [is needed or] is likely to be needed for any 'public purpose' [or for a company], a notification to that effect shall be published in the Official Gazette [and in daily newspapers circulating in that locality of which at least one shall be in the regional language] and a Collector shall cause public notice of the substance of such notification to be given at convenient places in the said locality [the last of the dates of such publications and the giving of such public notice, being hereinafter referred to as the date of the publications of the notifications].

Further Section 4(2) reads:

> Thereupon, it shall be lawful for any officer, either generally or especially authorised by such government in this behalf, and for his servants and the workmen, – to enter upon and survey and take levels of any land in such locality; to dig or bore into the sub-soil; to do all other acts necessary to ascertain whether the land is adapted for such purpose; to set out the boundaries of the land proposed to be taken and the intended line of the work [if any] proposed to be made thereon; to mark such levels, boundaries and line by placing marks and cutting trenches; and, where otherwise the survey cannot be completed and the levels taken and boundaries and line marked, to cut down and clear away any part of any standing crop, fence or jungle: provided that no person shall enter into any building or upon any enclosed court or garden attached to a dwelling house [unless with the consent of the occupier thereof] without previously giving such occupier at least seven days' notice in writing of his intention to do so.

Using these rigid Sections, Government has been forcibly acquiring lands in the name of 'public purpose'. An alarming scenario is the acquisition of agricultural lands for development projects. It is a fact that agricultural lands are being aggressively used for various projects and schemes of both the state and central governments.[32] Two issues further arise as a consequence of acquisition of land for 'public purpose'. On one hand is the immediate injury caused to the owners of the land, and second is the damaged caused in the aftermath of construction of development projects, both of which leads to destruction of agricultural land. Two illustrative examples are discussed in this regard. One pertains to the recent most case which concerns the acquisition of 519.843 acres of agricultural land for the construction of Industrial Growth Centre at Waiton, Chingarel, Imphal East District[33] and the second case relates to the submersion of 27,404.94 acres of agricultural land in three districts of Manipur as a result of commissioning of the Loktak Hydro Project at Komreikap in year 1994.

It is worthwhile to elaborate here that Growth Centres scheme was initiated in the Eight Plan by the Government of India with the aim of tackling the problem of regional imbalances in industrial development. As a model, large villages or small towns which have the potential to become the nuclei for the socio-economic development of the surrounding area are identified as Growth Centres. The Growth Centres can be identified by different orders with respect to the quality and the quantity of services and facilities, service area and population. A Growth Centre of lowest order should have services such as agricultural input centre, primary and middle school, maternity and child care centres and daily market. At the highest level, it must have manufacturing industries, hospitals, colleges and so on.

Idea of Growth Centres is situated within the understanding that with the doing away of the system of licensing of industries and coming into play of market forces, the industries tend to gravitate towards already developed areas which provide better infrastructure, easier availability of skilled workforce and forward and backward linkages in terms of availability of raw materials and markets for products. Growth Centres are, therefore, taken as special measures to promote development of industries in backward areas by policy makers.

Under the Growth Centre schemes, in year 2008, the Central Government approved an Industrial Growth Centre Project in Manipur at Lamlai, Napet at a project cost of INR 30.00 crore of which INR 15.00 crore will be the Government of India contribution, INR 5.00 crore as State Government contribution, INR 4.00 crore as loan and equity contribution from the financial institutions and INR 6.00 crore as loans and equity from other sources. A sum of INR 1.50 crore was sanctioned and released by the Government of India. However, there is no official notification defining the nature of the proposed Centre.

As a follow up to this proposal, site of proposed Centre was shifted. In a notification dated November 18, 2008, the Government of Manipur through the application of Land Acquisition Act 1894, authorised the concerned authority to acquire around 519.843 acres of agricultural land for the construction of Industrial Growth Centre at Waiton, Chingarel, Imphal East District. Ironical issue is that the Government 'knows' that the land to be acquired are agricultural land. For example, the same Gazette elaborates the Classification of the lands in question into two types such as *Anganphou* and *Phourel*.

A public notice served by the affected farmers read as follows:

> This is a very fertile land giving yield of around 1000 kg to 1400 kg per acre. Annual production of rice in this area is around 1,032,000 kg giving an annual income of around INR 2.27 crore from rice only. In

addition, from associated agricultural works such as weeding, transplantation, cutting and threshing etc. gives income to agricultural workers, annually, a total sum of around INR 6.20 lakhs. Income from hay and straw sums up to around INR 6.02 lakhs from this area of agricultural land. Furthermore, seasonal fish, vegetables and herbs are other benefits given to the people by this area of agricultural land (Waiton Mamang Chingarel Loukol Kanba Lup, 2008).

Following Table 5.14 illustrates the total number area proposed to be acquired by the State Government number of persons likely to be affected by the construction of the proposed Growth Centre.

Table 5.14: Schedule of land proposed to be acquired for Industrial Growth Centre, Chingarel

Area of agricultural land likely to be acquired (in acres)	*No. of pattadars likely to be affected*
519.843	339

Source: Government of Manipur. 2008. *Manipur Gazette*, 2008. No. 309, December 1, 1–26.

With regard to the second example, as per a Report conducted by the Committee of Experts, Constituted by the Government of Manipur, *vide* Order No. 25/15/99-Power (HC) dated December 22, 1999 submitted to the Gauhati High Court Imphal Bench in connection C.R. No. 32 of 1994, which was duly signed by Chief Engineer (Power), Government of Manipur, Chief Engineer (ICFD), Government of Manipur, Pr. Conservator of Forest, Government of Manipur, Director of Agriculture, Government of Manipur, Deputy Commissioner of Bishnupur, Imphal West and Thoubal, Joint Secretary (Power), Government of Manipur, and Commissioner Revenue, Government of Manipur, respectively, the estimated areas of land affected due to submersion by the Loktak Hydro-Electric Project is 27,404.94 acres of 12,129 *pattadars* (approximately). The district-wise affected area due to the commissioning of the Loktak Hydro Project at Komreikap in year 1994 is given as follows:

Table 5.15: District-wise affected area due to the commissioning of the Loktak Hydro Project at Komreikap in year 1994

District	*Area of land affected (in acres)*	*No. of pattadars affected (as on March 2006)*
Imphal West	8,818.75	3,109
Thoubal	11,989.57	5,978
Bishnupur	6,596.62	3,042
Total	**27,404.94**	**12,129**

Source: Government of Manipur. 2006. Report of the Committee of Experts constituted by the Government of Manipur (*vide* Orders No. 25/15/99-power (HC) dated 22/12/1999 in pursuance of the Hon'ble Gauhati High Court's Orders passed on 12/11/1999 in R.R. No. 32 of 1994) to examine loss and damage caused by Loktak Hydro-Electric Project. Imphal: Secretariat (Power Department). April 18: 4.

The Committee was of the view that since maintaining Loktak at certain predetermined level and/or in a manner controlled by the National Hydro-electric Power Corporation (NHPC) in order to enhance retention of water in the reservoir for generation of hydro electric power largely factored in the submersion of agricultural and other classes of lands around the lake, the Corporation, among others, has the onus to find ways and means to redress the grievances of the affected people on the one hand and to conserve the Loktak Wetland on the other. The Committee also felt that degradation of the catchment areas resulting in deposit of silt in Loktak over the years is another factor that has contributed to submersion of lands at the periphery of the Lake and loss to a large number of land owners and farmers. But the question is why the stake-holders, especially the NHPC, which has been exploiting the Loktak (reservoir) to generate hydro-electric power for more than two decades at minimum cost, did not invest the resources at their command, for the purpose of conservation/sustainable development of (the catchment areas of) Loktak Wetland—its ecology, bio-diversity, form and character (Government of Manipur, 2006: 5).

Table 5.16: Estimated value of average yield/loss per acre of 'Phourel' class of land

Items	*Value*	*Remarks*
Average yield/acre	1200 kg, i.e. 40 *Sangpais* of 30 kg each	*Sangpai* is the local term of measure of quantity
Value of yield/acre, i.e. 40 *Sangpais* @ Rs. 90 per *Sangpai* of 30 kg	INR 3,600.00	
Cost of cultivation/per acre	INR 1,760.00	
Net value of yield/acre, i.e. value of yield minus	INR 3,600 (–) INR 1,760.00 = INR 1,840.00	

Source: Government of Manipur, 2006. Report of the Committee of Experts constituted by the Government of Manipur (*vide* Orders No. 25/15/99-power (HC) dated 22/12/1999 in pursuance of the Hon'ble Gauhati High Court's Orders passed on 12/11/1999 in R.R. No. 32 of 1994) to examine loss and damage caused by Loktak Hydro-Electric Project. *Imphal: Secretariat (Power Department)*. April 18: 7.

Table 5.16 shows the average yield of rice per acre of land of the affected land, value of the yield, and cost of cultivation and so on to bring into knowledge the extent of damaged caused.

Here it is worthwhile to add that in spite of the visible damages that have come forth with the commissioning of a hydro project, Government of Manipur still has not learnt a lesson. Development is still understood in terms of large projects at the cost of land, gene pool of bio-diversity and human beings.

There are no available data on land diversion in Manipur.[34] However, it is an observable fact that agricultural lands are largely converted into homesteads, sites of private entrepreneurial sites, parking lots and so. This phenomenon

Table 5.17: Estimated value of average yield/loss per acre of '*Taothabi*' class of land

Items	*Value*	*Remarks*
Average yield/acre	1000 kg, i.e. 40 *Sangpais* of 25 kg each	*Sangpai* is the local term of measure of quantity
Value of yield/acre, i.e. 40 *Sangpais* @ INR 90 per *Sangpai* of 30 kgs	INR 2,600.00	
Cost of cultivation/per acre	INR 925.00	
Net value of yield/acre, i.e. value of yield minus	INR 2,600 (–) INR 925 = INR 1,675.00	

Source: Government of Manipur. 2006. Report of the Committee of experts constituted by the Government of Manipur (*vide* Orders No. 25/15/99-power (HC) dated 22/12/1999 in pursuance of the Hon'ble Gauhati High Court's Orders passed on 12/11/1999 in R.R. No. 32 of 1994) to examine loss and damage caused by Loktak Hydro-Electric Project. Imphal: Secretariat (Power Department). April 18: 7.

Box 5.1: Land Acquisition for Airport Expansion

250 farming families are protesting the acquisition of their fertile lands for modernisation of the Imphal airport. With cultivable land already at a premium in Manipur, the transition of agricultural land to infrastructure development all over the state will exacerbate the food crisis, add to poverty levels and cause loss of livelihoods.

Torn asunder for years by insurgency and limping development indices, Manipur is a tired state. Agriculture and allied activities like animal husbandry, horticulture, forestry and pisciculture, which engage 80 per cent of the workforce, are under threat from myopic development policies. And with non-agricultural activities having remained more or less at the household level of enterprise, Manipur's people face an uncertain future. Inevitably then, when the government sought to acquire 512 acres of land for modernisation and expansion of the runway at Imphal's Tulihal airport to international standards (as part of Ex-Prime Minister Manmohan Singh's special package for the state), there were widespread protests. On April 2, 2008, dissent against land acquisition reached a peak, and in a confrontation reminiscent of Nandigram, residents of villages that wil! be affected by the expansion — Malom, Ningombam, Meitram, Kodompokpi, Mongsangei and Konjeng Leikai — fought pitched battles with the police. Over the years since 1960, approximately 600 acres of arable land have been acquired already for the expansion of Tulihal airport.

Apart from the macro issue of marginalisation of agriculture at a time when a global food crisis looms large, the most important concern at the micro level in Manipur is scarcity of cultivable land. Spread over an area of 22,327 sq km,

(*Contd.*)

Manipur, which shares its northern, southern and western borders with Nagaland, Mizoram and Assam respectively and international borders with Myanmar on its eastern flank, has two distinct physical regions — a flat oval-shaped valley encompassing around 2,200 sq km of fertile land interspersed with wetlands, and an outlying hilly area. Farming in the hills, for obvious reasons, is largely subsistence, while cultivation in the valley is reasonably productive with many households augmenting their livelihood with horticulture and fish farming. The flatlands, however, comprise barely 10 per cent of the state's area and, due to its better accessibility and location of the state capital, Imphal is already under pressure from population and infrastructure expansion.

So, even if only 250-odd families, or 10,000 people, are displaced by the Tulihal expansion, in real terms, the human cost would be monumental, ranging from loss of ancestral property and secure livelihoods to ecological imbalance and impoverishment. Already Manipur's per capita income lags behind the national average, the state having swiftly changed from a subsistence economy, at the time of its accession to the Indian Union in 1949, to a reliant economy heavily dependent on imports of almost all essential commodities. "Any further alienation of land is likely to swell the ranks of the poor, and give a fillip to insurgency. As it is, many insurgent groups believe that shortsighted government policies have ignored the people's requirements," insists Deejen Khoisnam.

The government says loss of arable land will be compensated by a growth in tourism. State tourism minister T.N. Haokip told newsmen recently that an airport of international standards would help attract tourists and act as the launch pad for other tourism-related infrastructure development. Although tourism would be an easy sector to promote in a state that has some of the most beautiful locales in the country, a rich cultural heritage, endemic flora and fauna, the only floating sanctuary in the world (Keibul Lamjao National Park) and the largest freshwater lake in India (Loktak lake), the JAC remains unconvinced that a tourist-centric economy could ever make up for a reduction in production bases.

The JAC's grouse against the airport expansion move is based on several points. For one, it does not believe that the government is being entirely truthful in claiming that it needs more land for the runway's extension since the blueprint of the upgraded airport does not show one. Second, large tracts of land acquired earlier continue to be under the occupation of the security forces and the Central Public Works Department (CPWD) inside the airport premises; the government remains tight-lipped on the issue. Third, the government's argument that a bigger airport would help land essential commodities whose entry into Manipur, as of today, is hampered by frequent blockades and extortion on the highways by insurgent groups, is feeble. The state has three airports of which two are still under the control of the military. One of them could easily be used to land cargo planes. The government could also set up a highway protection force instead of tamely submitting to militancy. And, finally, as Khoisnam says: "The government could take a pointer from Mizoram and think of an airport in the sparsely populated hill area, where land use is optimal and human displacement minimal."

Source: Choudhuri, Monideepa, "Manipur resists land alienation", *InfoChange News & Features*, May 2008. http://infochangeindia.org/agriculture/features/manipur-resists-land-alienation.html

is not specific to the valley areas alone but also to the hill areas. Section 20 of the Manipur Land Revenue and Land Reforms Act 1960 with regard to diversion of land reads as follows:

> (1) If any person holding land for any purpose wishes to divert such land or any part thereof to any other purpose except agriculture, he shall apply for permission to the competent authority which may, subject to the provisions of this section and to the rules made under this Act, refuse permission or grant it on such conditions as it may think fit.
>
> (2) Permission to divert may be refused by the competent authority only on the ground that the diversion is likely to cause a public nuisance or that it is not in the interest of the general public or that the holder is unable or unwilling to comply with the conditions that may be imposed under sub-section 3.
>
> (3) Conditions may be imposed on diversion for the following objects and no others, namely in order to secure the public health, safety and convenience, and in the case of land which is to be used as building sites in order to secure, in addition, that the dimensions, arrangement and accessibility of the sites are adequate for the health and convenience of occupiers or are suitable to the locality.
>
> (4) If any land has been diverted without permission by the holder or by any other person with or without the consent of the holder, the competent authority, on receiving information thereof, may impose on the person responsible for the diversion a penalty not exceeding one hundred rupees, and may proceed in accordance with the provisions of sub-section (1) and if an application for permission to divert had been made.
>
> (5) If any land has been diverted in contravention of an order passed or of a condition imposed under any of

> the foregoing sub-section, the competent authority may serve a notice on the person responsible for such contravention, directing him, within a reasonable period to be stated in the notice, to use the land for its original purpose or to observe the condition; and such notice may require such person to remove any structure, to fill up any excavation, or to take such other steps as may be required in order that the land may be used for its original purpose, or that the condition may be satisfied. The competent authority may also impose on such person a penalty not exceeding one hundred rupees for such contravention, and a further penalty not exceeding four rupees for each day during which such contravention continues.

The purpose of citing elaborately sub-sections of the appropriate Section is to emphasise that there are stringent laws applicable with the protection of the agricultural land. Original intent of the Section is to rationalise revenue creation on land. However, current demand on land due to raising population, urbanization, and so makes it pertinent to utilize these sections of the land Act to protect agricultural land from diverting into other purposes. Refusal for diversion of agricultural land could be affirmatively done using sub-section 2 of Section 20 on the ground of 'public interest'; shortage of food grain is a public issue. Worrisome picture is the unavailability of records of land diversion due lapses on the side of the law implementing agencies.

Food Security *vis-à-vis* FTA

The full implementation of EU-India FTA will bring major structural shifts and impulses which will be detrimental to the food security of the state. The food deficiency of the state which is made through imports from the other state through PDS is going to be severely affected by the agreement as it will bring about intense liberalization and marginalized government role. Before going into the likely impact of the EU-India FTA on the food security of the state, let us go into the details of the likely requirement of food grains of the state in the next 10 years as it will inform about the tenacity and the seriousness of the situation. Table 5.18 gives the projection of population, food grains requirement, estimated food grain production and estimated deficit.

Table 5.18: Estimated Population and Rice Production, Rice Requirement and Deficit

(In thousand tonnes)

Year	*Population*	*Requirement*	*Production*	*Deficit (Case 1)*	*Deficit (Case 2)*
2012	2768570	534.33	403.0283	–131.03	–98.40
2013	2816190	543.52	404.5598	–138.96	–107.59
2014	2864628	552.87	406.0971	–146.77	–116.94
2015	2913900	562.38	407.6403	–154.74	–126.45
2016	2964019	572.06	409.1893	–162.87	–136.13
2017	3015000	581.89	410.7442	–171.15	–145.96
2018	3066858	591.09	412.3051	–179.59	–155.97
2019	3119608	602.08	413.8718	–188.21	–166.15
2020	3173265	612.44	415.4445	–197.00	–176.51
2021	3227845	622.97	417.0232	–205.95	–187.04

The population projection is calculated by taking the annual growth rate of population from 2001 to 2011 which is at about 1.72 per cent. The growth rate may even rise due to the influx of outsiders as consequence to the operation of FTA. The food grain requirement is calculated from the per capita yearly requirement of food grains as given by the Planning Commission which is 193 kg per capita per annum. The food grain production estimated using the growth rate attained in the last 8 years, i.e. 0.49 per cent. So by 2021 the food grain deficit of the state will cross the 200 thousand tonnes mark. So by 2021 the state will have food deficit for feeding its 10,67,098 people. Even we took the highest production in the last 10 years, i.e. 435.98 thousand tonnes, the estimated deficit is 187.04 thousand tonnes which is the yearly requirement of 9,69,119 people. We are assuming that the gross crop area is the same which is not a likely situation in the coming years looking at the prevailing situation. In other words the situation will be worst off owing to the existing rapid structural distortion in the agricultural sectors.

The state does not have draft agricultural policy, there is increasing urbanization with swelling population and shrinking agricultural land. Not only does the agricultural land, cultivable waste land also decreasing at a faster rate owe to massive construction work of the state. In 1990-91 the cultivable waste land was 1440 hectares and reduces to 740 hectares, a decrease of more than 50 per cent. So cultivable waste land is falling at a rate of 6.44 per cent per year, at this rate by now cultivable waste land would be 380 hectares. As the option of expanding agricultural land is cut off, the only available remedy will be intensive cultivation through a combination of modern inputs. But the available evidence on agriculture discusses above forecast a very gloomy picture and agrarian distress is looming large in the state. The situation calls for very active intervention from the state which will be a tale of despair in a regime of free trade. Important inputs like chemical fertilizers, weedicides, insecticides which have to be brought from other parts of India will be costlier day-by-day as subsidies provided to Indian farm sector are miniscule and will be reduced once the FTA set into motion.

The increased cost of production will discourage double cropping in paddy cultivation which is already felt since the past few years as the area sown more than once to total net sown area is 6.81 per cent in 2000-01. Paddy cultivation is done in *kharif* season and the scope of doing in *rabi* season is limited as it is less remunerative due to high cost and rampant marginalization of landholdings. So food security for the state in the coming years will be herculean task and state intervention is the ultimate tool. But in FTA regime, the Government will be obliging to the aspiration of EU-India FTA not to the immediate need of the people. In such a situation the most needed task of elevating to the status of food secure state is cut off.

Free Trade Agreement are carried to have a in depth penetration to the economy through influx of cheap goods and its ground work comes in the form of road expansion, enlargement of urban area, highway expansion, railway networks, airport expansion which ultimately lead to depletion of agricultural land which is more faster in the state like Manipur where there is limited agricultural land. With the increasing global penetration and inflows of cheap goods through the machines of FTA regime, there is as fast changing shift from 'production' economy to 'exchange' economy and as a result there has been transformation of the base of production, i.e. land are into other form which only smoothen (free) trade for instance agricultural land in the valley are converting into oil pumps, brick fields, hotels, godowns etc. which will be more heighten after the full operational of the EU-FTA. The cost of cultivation which is on an uninterrupted increase has discouraged cultivation which fuel by lethargic attitude from the government. The cumulative result will be the marginalization of the issue of food security in the state.

Moreover, in India there is apprehension of weakening of PDS system in India as consequences of the EU-India FTA. So, there is double trouble for Manipur as food grain deficiency is made up by this channel and on the other hand acceleration of food grain deficit of the state. The emerging scenario will be a grave threat to the food security of the state. If the situation persists like this, the state will heavily depend on the import of food grains from other regions and it means the people of the state will be heavily dependent on trade for our basic food security. So access to cheap, affordable and basic food grains will be under serious threat and incidence will be more on the poor and marginalized section which form the bulk of the population.

As discussed above, the components of food security — availability, accessibility and sustainability are not separate phenomenon, they are interrelated. Food security is linked to livelihood, food access and food consumption. Livelihood options or access in turn influences the demand for food and incentive for productions. Better livelihood access also leads to better life, better living, better education, better health and better absorption. Agriculture not only provides food but also the bulk of employment especially in rural areas. Agriculture being disturbed by the process of FTA means livelihood opportunity of the majority at stake. Deprivation of livelihood means the other important objectives of food security such as accessibility and sustainability will be a far cry. Even if there is availability of food grain, low purchasing power as a result of low quality of unemployment or loss of livelihood will derail the core of the food security. In this situation, there are only two ways in which the food security can be ensured. First, government directly supplying food grains at a subsidized rate and secondly, expanding the employment opportunity and livelihood options through sectoral development. Both of which are not a easy task looking at the existing scenario and will not be a conducive one during the FTA regime.

For analyzing likely impact of FTA on the employment structure and livelihood patterns, the study will use the concept of population census data which are available decennially. The population census data used three concepts of workers—main workers, marginal workers and non-workers. The main worker was defined as a person whose main activity was participation in any economically productive work by his physical and mental activities and who had worked for 183 days or more in a year. A marginal worker is defined as a person whose main activity was participation in any economically production work by his physical or mental activity for less than 183 days. A non-worker is defined as a person who had not done any work at any time. From 1981 Census these concepts were in use.

Table 5.19: Composition of workforce

(As percentage of population)

Type of workers	*1981*	*1991*	*2001*
Main workers	40.3	38.6	30.4
Marginal workers	2.1	3.6	13.2
Non-workers	54.1	57.3	58.2

Source: Census of India 1981, 1991, 2001.

From Table 5.19 it is observed the percentage of main workers is declining and is more pronounced in 2001. On the other hand, marginal workers also show an increasing trend and are more rapid during 1991 and 2001. The non-workers increase marginally during the period. The period 1991 and 2001 marks the liberalization phase and it witnessed increasing marginalization of employment. The structural changes brought about by liberalization has reduced the opportunity of engaging as a main worker and only resulted in accelerated marginalization. In other words, workers are unable to sustain their livelihood as result of the penetration of external elements in the economy and such situation will be more intense in a FTA regime. The sex-wise and activity-wise break up will give a more meaningful picture. Tables 5.20 and 5.21 show the sex-wise distribution of workers and main workers by industrial categories.

Table 5.20: Distribution of Workers by Sex

Type of worker	*1991*	*2001*	*Per cent rise/decline*
Main workers	708283	659364	–6.9
Male	414812	430277	3.6
Female	293471	229137	–22
Marginal Workers	66621	285849	329
Male	9958	96984	873
Female	56663	188860	233

Source: Same as Table 5.19.

Table 5.21: Main Workers by Industrial Categories

Type of Workers	*1991*	*2001*	*Per cent rise/decline*
Cultivator	437499	285809	–34.67
Male	243267	174864	–28.11
Female	194232	110940	–42.88
Agricultural labourer	47350	41819	–11.68
Male	19151	25837	32.56
Female	28199	16432	–41.72
Man., Pro., repa.	57433	43163	–24.84
Male	17293	14337	–17
Female	40140	28826	–28.18
Other Services	166001	288573	73
Male	135101	215634	59.60
Female	30900	72939	136

Note: Man., Pro., repa. Means manufacturing, processing and repairing.
Source: Same as table 5.19.

Table 5.20 gives the distribution of main and marginal workers by sex. It is observed that main workers decline by 6.9 per cent. But the male main workers increases by 3.6 per cent and female shows a 22 per cent decline. For marginal workers, it shows a gigantic rise, i.e. 329 per cent and it has been more intense in male (873%) then female (233%). Even though male marginal workers have increased more than that of female, absolute number of female marginal workers has doubled as compared to male. The incidence of liberalization has been more on female workers as female's economic and social positions are weaker and a harshly competitive atmosphere hurts the weakest the most. An FTA regime will make the situation more intense. Looking at the activity-wise category of main workers, all the industrial categories except for other services has declined and the highest being the cultivators followed by manufacturing, processing and repairing services. The decrease in cultivator is not the result of agriculture becoming productive per worker but due to intrinsic weakness of the agriculture as discussed above. In all categories that have shown a declining trend, female workers have declined more than male workers (except for agricultural labourer where male have shown positive increase). The only categories that have shown increase is the other services where female has exceeded male workers, but male absolute number is triple times that of female workers. Employment pattern and livelihood option in the post liberalization phase has been deteriorated for both male and female but more pronounced in female and FTA regime will bring more of such unfriendly atmosphere as FTAs are 'high degree' liberalizations. Agriculture which carries bulk of both food security and livelihood (more than 50% of working population are engaged in agriculture) is under grave threat owing to evolving structural distortion and political economy shaping in the state and situation will be more worst with the onset of FTA like that of EU-India which are taken in the interest of MNCs not necessarily for the common people.

Conclusion

Issue of food security is a matter of pertinent concern, not only for Manipur but also for the entire world. The India-EU FTA is expected to have a significant impact on livelihoods, access to food and productive resources in the state, especially for the poor and marginalised. The lack of transparency and adequate consultation with all stakeholders, especially vulnerable groups like farmers, indigenous groups, women, patients' groups, and micro, small and medium enterprises, during the FTA negotiation process has been a consistent worry to civil society organisations and development policy analysts. In India, neither the draft text nor the impact assessment studies have been shared with stakeholders, State Governments or with civil society, and nor is there any form of parliamentary oversight. That such an important policy measure can be introduced without transparent and extensive consultations with stakeholders undermines Indian democracy.

In terms of the EU's trade policy, a joint perusal of CAP

and the demands made in its FTAs with developing countries will throw into serious doubt its claims of being supportive of sustainable development in the Third World. The EU's insistence on including agriculture belies the European Commission's claims that agriculture is not a major issue in the negotiation. It is clear that the EU recognizes that it is a hugely sensitive sector for India in terms of its livelihood and food security implications, but is still continuing with aggressive demands in this sector. Whether, the Indian Government will give up its policy of pursuing self-sufficiency in agriculture and food, even in the presence of a rapidly exploding food crisis which is bound to recur more often than before, remains to be seen.

Notes

1. Priyoranjan Chongtham, "Agrarian Structure and Production Relations in Manipur", *Unpublished Ph.D. Thesis,* Manipur University. 2005, 27.
2. *Ibid.*
3. R.Brown, *Statistical Account of Manipur*, (New Delhi: Mittal Publications, 2001).
4. R.B. Pemberton, *Eastern Frontier of India,* (New Delhi: Mittal Publications, 1979).
5. Manipur Administrative Report for the year 1939-40.
6. Disturbance at Imphal, December 1939; Confidential File, Manipur State Archive.
7. Manipur Administrative Report for the year 1939-40.
8. "They (women protestors) surrounded them (Captain Stone's men) and tried to snatch the rifles from their hands and men in the background threw stones"; Letter from the Commandant, 4th Battalion, AR, Imphal to the Political Agent in Manipur: Letter no. 2014/ IV-18 (B) dated 13th December, 1939.
9. Press Communiqué.
10. Disturbance at Imphal, December 1939.
11. There were as many as 18 mills operating in the state in 1939 and most of the political thinkers felt that these mills "with a daily outturn of 11,200 mounds of rice, absorb all the available paddy in the state thereby creating unemployment amongst the women"; Resolution passed by Manipur Praja Sanmelini. They considered that mills

consumed thousands of maunds of paddy daily, which suggested throwing out of employment the masses that lived by husking, thus perpetuating problem of unemployment in Manipur; Resolution passed by Manipur Praja Sanmelini. 7th sitting: Police Bazar Field; 2 pm. 7-1-40.

12. Manipur Administrative Report for the year 1939-40.
13. *Ibid.*
14. *Ibid.*
15. It is recorded that "in the case of three women the injuries were rather severe. A woman, Oinam Ibemahan by name was subjected to the most inhuman treatment by the police members of the Durbar (the 2nd son of the King) who kicked her in the private parts, as the result of which the women fell down senseless and bleeding; Irabot's letter."
16. Miss. Mayanglambam Kunjeshwari, *The Women Movements in Manipur*, M. Phil. Dissertaion, Manipur University. 1992, pp. 42, 65.
17. A. Balkrishna Sharma, *Irabot and his time: a brief History of Colonial Manipur, Based on the Biography of Neta Hijam Irabot.* National Research Centre (NRC) library, Imphal, p. 13.
18. Manipur Administrative Report for the year 1907-1908.
19. Manipur Administrative Report for the year 1915-1916.
20. *Ibid.*
21. Manipur Administrative Report for the year 1935-36.
22. Manipur Administrative Report for the year 1909-10.
23. Manipur Administrative Report for the year 1937-38.
24. Manipur Administrative Report for the year 1935-36.
25. Indebtedness had crept in since 1916 and at the close of the year 1923-24 the state was indebted to Government to the extent of Rs. 268750; Manipur Administrative Report for the year 1923-24.
26. "Marwaris in the business atmosphere of Manipur meant exploitation in every available products of the state, at the expense of your humble subjects—who have no capital and resources enough to compete with them in their new struggle. Thus they are left in a critical position—to choose either their own destruction or the thralldom of the Marwari capitalists—who eat up every moment into the entrails of the state"; Application to the judicial members, Manipur State Durbar. 28 September, 1920. By Manipur State Subjects for redressing the wrongs they suffered at the hands of the Marwaris.
27. Planning Commission, *Manipur State Development Report* (New Delhi: Institute for Human Development, 2006), 109.
28. Planning Commission, *Manipur State Development Report*, 100.
29. Government of Manipur, *Draft Annual Plan, 2007-08,* Department of Agriculture, 2008.
30. Bruce F. Johnston and P. Kilbey, "'Unimodal' and 'bimodal' strategies of agrarian change" *Rural Development: Theories of Peasant Economy*

and Agrarian Change, John Harris ed. (London: Hutchinson & Co. Ltd., 1982), 53.

31. Government of Manipur, *Draft Annual Plan*, 4.
32. N. Manichandra Singh, "*Foodgrain Economy and Food Security*" *Quest for Development in Manipur: Continuity Constraints and Contradictions*, Homen Thangjam and H. Isworchandra Sharma eds., New Delhi: Concept Publishing Co., (P.) Ltd., 2013, 67-93.
33. Government of Manipur (2008) *Manipur Gazette 309*, December 1, i-xxiv.
34. *Manipur Land Revenue and Land Reforms Act, 1960* states, 'Diversion' in this (section) means using land assessed to one purpose for any other purpose, but using land for the purpose of agriculture where it is assessed with reference to any other purpose shall not be deemed to be 'diversion'.

6

Conclusion

The study has identified key areas of concern, which have the potential to be affected as a consequence of the proposed India-EU FTA. Trade and investment, hydropower, mining, oil exploration and drilling and agriculture have been given prime focus in the study. Apart from the model of development initiated in the state dictated primarily by exogenous factors and movers, which does take into account local needs and aspiration, the study has also highlighted militarization and securitization of both trade and development in the state. Two processes that have informed development initiatives have been identified as reproduction of the British colonial policies after merging with India and the centrality of security in any development doctrines and policies as far the North east region as a whole is concerned. These have largely led to underdevelopment of the region. Although there has been shift in the perception of the policy makers as far as the region is concerned from the early 1990s, from a region inaccessible, hostile terrain and that no development can take place, to a land of opportunity and Gateway to the East, centrality of security has never been abandoned. The change in the perception was dictated by changes taking place around the world, in terms of geo-politics, after the end of the Cold War, and Structural Adjustment Programme (SAP) undertaken by India for its liberalization and privatization drive. Thus, the

North east became strategically important for India's Look East Policy.

But as witnessed from the experience of the Indo-Myanmar Border Trade, as a part of the LEP, Manipur has not benefited from the ongoing trade. Formal trade is as good as non-existent, illegal trade thrives in spite of presence of numerous security forces along the highway. In fact, the intrusion of Chinese made cheap goods have resulted in destruction of traditional industries, in an already backward state with a weak manufacturing base. This has made Manipur as a transit route, nothing else. Attempts at formalization of trade have resulted in displacement of the traders, such as the women-folk of Manipur, who were at the fore of trade and commerce since historical times, and who practiced Moreh Trade to sustain livelihood. At a deeper level, the trade has not benefited Manipur in two senses. First, in the identified list of tradable goods, there are no locally produced goods, such as products of handloom and handicraft and others. Secondly, just as the traditional women-Moreh-traders have been displaced, there is no substantive participation in the trade by local traders, largely on account of lack of capital, expertise and bottlenecks prevalent in getting licences. In such a scenario, other than providing secondary and tertiary services, one can say that there is no involvement of the local population in the Indo-Myanmar border trade, and thus, no benefits. Further, the study has also highlighted that the Indo-Myanmar Trade is a guise to fight insurgency in the region. This has been corroborated by the fact that the border trade has not improved while viewed within the context of the overall trade between India and Myanmar.

Viewed behind this background, the proposed India-EU FTA, is bound to maximize the environment of militarization and further the destruction of local industry.

Harnessing water energy, as elucidated by the experiences in Manipur, such the Tipaimukh and others show, militarizes the civilian space and leads to displacement and environmental destruction. North east presents as a viable area where potentials for investment exist for EU and others. Even if a company has received environmental clearance, there needs to be safeguards, which does not allow the same to blame local population as has been shown by the experience of the Loktak Lake.

As far as mining and oil exploration and extraction are concerned Union laws can easily bypass state legislations. As we have seen in the case of Odisha and Meghalaya, the Union laws override state legislation. The case of Meghalaya is merits attention. Mining at low scale has been a traditional practice of the indigenous people in the state, which it state legislations recognizes. At the same time, customary laws related with landownership and lease is a legislated piece of legal safeguard in the state unlike Manipur. In spite of the existence of such laws, Lafarge could come out victorious. Compared to Manipur and Odisha, Manipur is at a fragile state, both in terms of absence of laws as well as given the votility of the social composition of population. As of now, conflict originating from mineral resources has not taken place in Manipur. On the brighter side, communities, irrespective of tribe and ethnic affiliations came out together to oppose the move against oil exploration and drilling by Reliant Energy. However, the proposed Inida-EU FTA is likely to exacerbate displacement and dispossession of the peoples' right to own resources and conserve them. The FTA is likely to weaken of existing legislative safeguards such as laws related with lease, rental and ownership. It would also entail influx of skilled non-local labourers and deny work opportunities to the natives. This is a worrisome aspect when viewed at the background of illegal influx and demographic shifts in the state.

Finally, information related with ores and metals are closely guarded, given the tag of national wealth. What puts Manipur at stake is that apart from information partially made public, there can be no access to information on the availability of ores, minerals and metals. Thus, other than, these public materials, others, such as availability of uranium, and plans for investment from willing parties, are kept as confidential. Given the closely guarded nature of the negotiations related with the proposed India-EU FTA, one is not sure if already plans are afoot for investment in these sectors.

The full implementation of EU-India free trade will bring major structural shifts and impulses which will be detrimental to the food security of the state. The food deficiency of the state which is made through imports from the other state through PDS is going to be severely affected by the agreement as it will emphasise more on role of private players and reduce government role. The study shows that by 2021 the food grain deficit of the state will cross the 200 thousand tonnes. So by 2021 the state will have food deficit for feeding a population of about 10,67,098 people. Even we took the highest production in the last 10 years, i.e. 435.98 thousand tonnes, the estimated deficit is 187.04 thousand which is the yearly requirement of 9,69119 people.

Food security is linked to livelihood, food access and food consumption. Livelihood options or access in turn influences the demand for food and incentive for productions. Better livelihood access also leads to better life, better living, better education, better health and better absorption. Agriculture not only provides food but also the bulk of employment especially in rural areas. Agriculture being disturbed by the process of FTA means livelihood opportunity of the majority at stake. Deprivation of livelihood means the other important objectives of food security such as accessibility and sustainability will be a far cry. Even if there is availability of food grain, low purchasing power as a result of low quality of unemployment or loss of livelihood will derail the core of the food security. In this situation, there are only two ways in which the food security can be ensured. First, government directly supplying food grains at a subsidized rate and secondly, expanding the employment opportunity and livelihood options through sectoral development. Both of which is not a easy task looking at the existing scenario and will not be a conducive one during the FTA regime.

With regard to employment, the study has shown that even though male marginal workers has increased more than that of female, absolute number of female marginal workers has doubled as compared to male. The incidence of liberalization has been more on female workers as female's economic and social positions are weaker and a harshly competitive atmosphere hurts the weakest the most. An FTA regime will make the situation more intense. Employment pattern and livelihood option in the post liberalization phase has been deteriorated for both male and female but more pronounced in female and FTA regime will bring more of such unfriendly atmosphere as FTAs are 'high degree' liberalizations. Agriculture which carries bulk of both food security and livelihood is under grave threat owing to evolving structural distortion and political economy shaping in the state and situation will be more worst with the onset of FTA like that of EU-India which are taken in the interest of MNC not necessarily for the common people.

Recommendations

Resistance against trade liberalization and the proposed India-EU FTA has been going on in India. However, the situation in the North east demands separate treatment and different form of resistance. For one, opposition to the India-EU FTA has largely originated from specific stakeholders such as from organised pharmaceutical associations, automobile and automotive manufacturers, retail, dairy and organized farmers, and so on. Bargaining and preservation of trade interests form the basis of resistance, and by this merit find a platform for negotiation with the concerned party. But on the other hand, the North east or Manipur experiences an altogether existential paradigm, for example, living amidst the reality of armed conflict situation, and so far away from the hold of companies. Mostly, in the case of North east, resistance has been about a collective good. In this sense, it is more about conservation of local resources, environmental preservation and protecting the rights of the people. Therefore, the terms of engagement has to be of a different configuration, so thus, the mode of resistance and formation of network with other organizations. In the light of the scenario of militarization and human rights situation as well as narratives from the few development (and trade) experiences in Manipur, the study recommends that the proposed India-EU FTA needs take into account the following:

- At the policy level, there should be clauses to address issues of human rights violations as per norms of the United Nations.
- India-EU should seek free, fair and prior informed consent of the people in the region as endorsed in the ILO Convention, the UN Declaration on Rights of the Indigenous People and others before taking up any trade agreement related to land, mountain, forest, water, minerals, hydrocarbons etc. which are traditionally owned by the indigenous people.
- In the case of Manipur, specific legislations are recommended, related with land, i.e. revising the existing the state acts on land, legislation of customary laws and keeping them within the purview of the local Government.
- There should be a mechanism for sharing of the earning from the resources with the people of Manipur.
- The Government of India should clearly define the link between trade and non-trade issues such as political conflict and human rights issues as violation of human rights in the region is grave.
- There should be a strong mechanism to ensure social and environmental standard and as such systematic Environmental Impact Assessment (EIA) has to be conducted for any exploration works.

- In addition to EIA, there has to be safeguards to make the errant bodies pay, when harm is identified, even after a project has duly completed.
- There is no plan for relocation of the indigenous people who are going to be displaced from their traditional land. Thus, rehabilitation and resettlement should be done before commencing the exploration work.
- It is worth to mention here that rehabilitation and resettlement (R&R) for the displaced people due to any kind of developmental project is mandatory, however, no R&R has been done properly for those projects which are already completed.

APPENDICES

Appendix-I

Memorandum of Understanding

THIS MEMORANDUM OF UNDERSTANDING is signed BETWEEN The Indian Trade Delegation represented by **Shri M. Chandrakishore Singh, North East Federation on International Trade (NEDFIT), Manipur Chapter** AND Myanmar Trade Delegation represented by **U Hla Maung, President, Union of Myanmar Border Trade Chamber of Commerce (UMBTCC)**, Tamu (Myanmar), on this 17th May, 2010 on the occasion of Two-Day Buyer Seller-*cum*-Ground Level Officials Meet.

WHEREAS the trade organizations after detailed discussions decided to lay down the following agreement to strengthen and enhance, economic, trade and investment activities for promotion of trade in goods and services as well as create a transparent, liberal and sincere regimes to explore new areas and develop appropriate measures for closer economic co-operation between the parties, the following broad agreements were made:

1. That at Myanmar and India border, Myanmar authorized Immigration Department to allow the Indian Businessmen for entry into Myanmar territory issuing **Border Pass** from morning 6.00 am to evening

6.00 pm (MST). This border pass ticket is invalid if the businessman return back to India Territory. Such Border Pass may be validated for 7 (seven) days especially for businessmen. Authority of Myanmar shall be requested.

2. That exchange of traditional cultural troupe of Manipur and other North Eastern States (India) and Myanmar at the convenient time to strengthen bilateral ties of friendship shall be considered by both sides if required necessary permission shall also be obtained.
3. That as an initiative for promotion of tourism. The trade delegates of Manipur or North Eastern States of India, visits to Mandalay in Myanmar by Indian delegates and to Guwahati and other North Eastern States of India for the Myanmar delegates shall be affected to promote trade and people-to-people contact.
4. That UMBTCC and NEDFIT, Manipur Chapter have agreed in principle to request the respective country Government for facilitation of **Visa on Arrival** at Tamu-Moreh border points.
5. That Indian side and Myanmar side may consider for allowing movement of export-import cargo/vehicles up to warehouse on both sides which was considered during the visit of Indian Inter-Ministerial Team on 9/11/2009 to Tamu.
6. That the two sides agreed to exchange lists of prospective traders of both sides within May 2010 or whichever is earlier.
7. That the privilege of weighing the export-import consignment in the Land Customs Station, Moreh constructed under ASIDE Scheme of Ministry of Commerce, Government of India may be taken by both sides.
8. That the Food Safety norms of International Rules and Regulations may be adopted for which the

NEDFIT shall supply a copy of the Handbooks/Rules and Regulations to UMBTCC at the earliest.

9. That to facilitate import-export of fish and livestock, operational of animal quarantine office may be considered by both sides.
10. The import of rice by Indian side shall be started at the earliest to help the shortage of rice faced by State of Manipur and North Eastern States.
11. That Indian side may be allowed to open more number of banks at the border town as well as at Yangon as the present designated bank of UBI is unable to cater the need of traders for operational L/C facility.
12. That both sides may extend mutual co-operational of Imphal to Mandalay Bus Service.
13. That State Government of Manipur or Indian side shall request the Supreme Court of India to lift the ban on import of timber from Myanmar through the North East States. The NEDFIT, Manipur Chapter shall coordinate with different NE States and other agencies and it shall move the High Powered Committee constituted by Supreme Court to effect necessary changes in this regard in the interest of the NE region.
14. That to facilitate and promote game and sports, a friendly football match shall be arranged at Tamu and Imphal for the boys and girls of both sides within the winter season of 2010 subject to approval of appropriate authorities.
15. That holding of regular **Buyer Seller and Ground Level Officials Meet** of both the countries will definitely speed up the development of bilateral trade. That such meeting will enable the authorities on both sides to articulate their problems, evolve collective and appropriate solutions and implements them. Most important aspects of such meeting are to settle trade discrepancies/misunderstanding/disputes of both sides and to bring amicable solutions. The **Meet** to be held

in every 6 (six) months to help the traders, guide them to develop, disseminate and share business information among the authorities on one side and traders/ entrepreneurs on the other.

Signed on 17/05/2010 at Water World Restaurant Hall of Tamu, Sagaing Division, Myanmar in presence of officials from both the countries in two originals in English language.

For	For
UMBTCC	**NEDFIT, Manipur Chapter**
(U Hla Maung)	(M. Chandrakishore Singh)
	President
	President, Manipur Chapter

In presence of:-

(U San New Win)

Director,
Border Trade Department,
The Union of Myanmar.

(T. Pamei, IAS)
Director of Commerce and Industries,
Government of Manipur

(Bijoy Phangcho)
Working President,
NEDFIT

Appendix-II

Recommendations of the Moreh Chamber of Commerce, Moreh

The Moreh Chamber of Commerce, Moreh is bound to recommend the following suggestions/comments after a minute discussion on the past and present trend of Trade:

1. The Export and Import activities in the Indo-Myanmar Border Trade is not up to the mark rather declining day-by-day to a number of reasons, a few point is as below:
   Trade in the barter and exchange mechanism is restricted to only 22 items. Trade(s) who want to import commodities from Myanmar suffer dearth/ scarcity of commodities to export, whereas highly demanded goods which are not enlisted in the 22 items, viz. motorcycle, textiles, medicines, bi-cycles, cosmetics, sandal-woods and their parts, manure etc. are exported illegally.
   Therefore, the 22 items needed review, and items on demand should be included.

   Obstruction by the Anti-social Element

   To initiate a peaceful fruitful dialogue with any group of people whose activity is associated with anti-socialism might not be conventional. It may go beyond the framework of our constitutional and general ethics of Border Trade. So, handling with them may be convenient with the help of some other 3rd party as to bring to a feasible negotiation.

2. The Central Government makes amendment in the classification of Export and Import items from time to time as Free Trade Policy. Obviously, almost all commodities of Myanmar Origin are permitted, excepting third country goods, to import through the border. But in reality, as far as volume of goods imported and amount expended to Myanmar is concern goods of the third country dominates by 70 per cent of the imported goods (including Electronic items, Blankets. Household items from China, Japan, and Thailand etc.). It may be assumed that the total amount in purchasing the goods of third country as 500 crores annually, and for which extortion money is collected by the personnel of different Government Department(s).

   As authorities of Myanmar have no restriction in trading the 3rd countries' goods meanwhile buyers/traders demand the same highly; here comes the point where Government Department(s) practicing extortion in bulk for their own pocket.

   It can be checked by making a State Trade Policy legalizing the trading of third countries' goods, empowering Local trade bodies. As consequence it may enhance the state income not less than 5 (five) crores annually, transact the traders' business peacefully, settle goods and their cost effectiveness regularly and help the Government machineries deployed to develop a good moral atmosphere by discharging their duties up to the mark.

3. It is very much necessary to open a market at Moreh where all the goods items found at Nanphalong (Myanmar) Market should be made available at a price almost equal to that of Nanphalong, and goods of India origin may in exposition.

So as to survive the market in practical working hours for marketing in Nanphalong by the Indian buyers may be scheduled to either before noon or after noon.

4. Keeping the reduction of cost effectiveness for items, and mutual co-operation and understanding among the traders of both countries for the development of the Border trade, in mind Free movement by the citizens traders of both countries up to some specific points, namely from Moreh to Mandalay and Tamu to Guwahati *vice versa* along with items of goods should be allowed.
5. The practices of extortion of illegal Taxes at least by the Government machineries mainly Manipur Police, Customs at different gates should be reduced/stopped, and the No. of check gates should be reduced.
6. Traders/Buyers from different parts of the countries should be managed to get aid/guidance through a responsible trade-body well equipped by the Government (State).
7. For construction of composite check post the most feasible point is in and around Kondong Lairembi because all roads converge at this point.

I, on behalf of the Chamber of Commerce, submit the above few suggestion/comments, and pray you to extend Mutual co-operations for the betterment of the border trade.

With Regards

Dated: 08/11/06
Moreh

I. Rajendra Singh
Representative
Moreh Chamber of Commerce,
Moreh

Appendix-III

Agreement between the Government of the Republic of India and the Government of the Union of Myanmar of Border Trade Between the Two Countries

The Government of the Republic of India and the Government of the Union of Myanmar, being desirous of promoting trade relations India and Myanmar and through friendly consultations have agreed to the formal establishment of border trade on the basis of equality and mutual benefit and have reached the following Agreement:

ARTICLE I

The border Trade shall be conducted through the following designated customs posts and in accordance with the laws, regulations and procedures in force in either country:

(a) Moreh in India and Tamu in Myanmar;
(b) Champai in India and Rih in Myanmar; and
(c) Other places that may be notified by mutual agreement between the two countries.

Adequate provisions will be made to enable buyers of either country to inspect and take delivery of goods at the customs posts in the country of the seller.

The goods to be traded on the border under this agreement shall be as permitted by both Governments.

ARTICLE II

Exchange of locally produced commodities as indicated in Annexure-I, by people living along both sides of the Indo-Myanmar border will continue as per the prevailing customary practice including the barter mechanism.

ARTICLE III

Trade under this Agreement may be conducted in freely convertible currencies or in currencies mutually agreed upon by the two countries, including through counter trade agreements.

ARTICLE IV

This Agreement shall be reviewed periodically by both sides to ensure successful implementation of its objectives and provisions. In case of difference relating to and arising out of this agreement, the same shall be amicably settled in the spirit of mutual cooperation and friendship.

ARTICLE V

Amemdment(s) and /or supplement(s) to this agreement shall be made by Exchange of Letters between the two sides.

ARTICLE VI

This Agreement shall come into force with effect from a date mutually agreed upon by the two sides and shall remain in forces two years from date. It shall be automatically extend for a period of two years at a time unless either side gives notice in writing of its intention to terminate this Agreement three months in advance of the date of expiry.

Done in New Delhi on the 21st day of January, 1994 in three originals, in Hindi, Myanmar and English Languages.

The three texts shall be equally authentic, but in case of any divergence of interpretation, the English text shall prevail.

On behalf of the Government of India	*On behalf of the Republic of the Union of Myanmar*
Sd/-	*Sd/-*
(Tejendra Khanna)	**(Lt. Colonel Kyaw Myint)**
Secretary	*Director General, Directorate of Trade,*
Ministry of Commerce	*Ministry of Trade*

Bibliography

A. Archival Material

Manipur Administrative Report for the year 1907-08, Imphal: Manipur State Archives.
Manipur Administrative Report for the year 1909-10, Imphal: Manipur State Archives.
Manipur Administrative Report for the year 1915-16, Imphal: Manipur State Archives.
Manipur Administrative Report for the year 1935-36, Imphal: Manipur State Archives.
Manipur Administrative Report for the year 1937-38, Imphal: Manipur State Archives.

B. Books

Batra, Ravi (1993), *The Myth of Free Trade*, New York: Charles Scribner's Sons & Macmillan Publishing Company.
Baumol, William and Blinder, Alan (2012), *Economics: Principles and Policy*, International Edition: South-Western CENGAGE Learning.
Boudreaux, Don (2007), *Globalization*, Westport, Connecticut & London: Greenwood Press.
Brakman, Steven, Harry Garretsen, Charles Van Marrewijk and Arjen Van Witteloostuijn (2006), *Nations and Firms in the Global Economy: An Introduction to International Economics and Business*, Cambridge: Cambridge University Press.
Brown, Robert (2001), *Statistical Account of Manipur*, New Delhi: Mittal Publications.

Chongtham, Priyoranjan (2005), *Agrarian Structure and Production Relations in Manipur*, Ph.D. Thesis, Manipur University.

Clay, Henry (1843), *The Life and Speeches of Henry Clay, II*, California: University of California Libraries.

Dixit, J.N. (2001), *Indian Foreign Policies and its Neighbours*, New Delhi: Gyan Books.

Forum for Indigenous Perspectives and Action (2007), *The Negation of Indigenous Peoples Territory: The Case of Lafarge Cement in Meghalaya, NE India*, Imphal: FIPA.

Friedman, Milton (1962, 2002), *Capitalism and Freedom*, Chicago: University of Chicago Press.

Government of India, *Transforming the Northeast: Tackling Backlogs in Basic Minimum Services and Infrastructural Needs*, New Delhi: Planning Commission, March 7, 1997.

Government of Manipur, *Draft Annual Plan, 2007-08*, Imphal: Department of Agriculture, 2008.

Government of Manipur, *Draft Industrial Policy of Manipur*, Imphal, 2011.

Government of Manipur, *Industrial Policy of Manipur*, Imphal, 1996.

Gray, John (1998), *False Dawn: The Delusions of Global Capitalism*, New York: The New Press.

Haluk, Serdar (1997), *A Microeconomic Analysis of Slavery in Comparison to Free Labor*, Ankara: Bilkent University.

Institute for Human Development (2006), *Manipur State development Report*, New Delhi: Planning Commission of India.

Johnston, Bruce F. and P. Kilbey (1982), "'Unimodal' and 'bimodal' strategies of agrarian change" in John Harris (ed.), *Rural Development: Theories of Peasant Economy and Agrarian Change*, London: Hutchinson & Co..

Keynes, John Maynard (1936, 1997), *The General Theory of Employment, Interest, and Money*, New York: Prometheus.

Kunjeshwari, Mayanglambam (1992), *The women movements in Manipur*, M. Phil. Dissertation, Canchipur: Manipur University.

Marx, Karl and Engels, Friedrich (1974), *The Civil War in the United States*, Internat. Publ.

Naraya, Deepa (2000); Patel, Raj; Schafft, Kai; Rademacher, Anne & Koch-Schulte, Sarah, *Voices of the Poor: Can Anyone Hear Us?* New York: Oxford University Press.

Pemberton, R.B. (1979), *Eastern Frontier of India*, New Delhi: Mittal Publications.

Robbins, Richard H. (2011), *Global Problems and the Culture of Capitalism*, Boston: Pearson, (5th edition).

Sharma, A. Balkrishna (2000), *Irabot and His Time: A Brief History of Colonial Manipur*, Imphal: National Research Centre.

Singh, N. Manichandra (2013), "Foodgrain Economy and Food Security", in Homen Thangjam & H. Isworchandra Sharma (eds.), *Quest for Development in Manipur: Continuity Constraints and Contradictions*, New Delhi: Concept Publishing Co. (P) Ltd.

Smith, Adam (1776, 2000), *The Wealth of Nations*, New York: Modern Library.

Smith, J.W. (1994), *The World's Wasted Wealth 2: Save Our Wealth, Save Our Environment*, California: Institute for Economic Democracy.

Stiglitz, Joseph (2002), *Globalization and its Discontents*, New York: Penguin Books.

Stroup, Richard, Gwartney, James and Sobel, Russell (2013), *Economics: Private and Public Choice*, International Edition: South-Western CENGAGE Learning.

C. Journals & Articles

Yumnam, Amar, "Development Intervention in the Northeast: A Critique", *Eastern Quarterly*, Vol. 3, Issue III, October-December, 2005.

Churchill, Laishram "Manipur's Economy: Trajectory and Transformation Before and During the British Period", *Alternative Perspectives*, Vol. III, No. 3, March – June, 2006.

Public Citizen, "NAFTA Truth and Consequences: Corn", accessed on January 1, 2013 (www.citizen.org/trade/:article_redirect.cfn?ID:11330).

Sachdeva, Gulshan, "India EU Economic Linkages: Need to Broaden Strategic Partnership", *International Studies*, Vol. 45, No. 4, 2008.

Samom, Sobhapati, "Chromite mining project opposed by Manipur bodies", *The Assam Tribune*, Guwahati, Wednesday, October 22, 2008.

Wessel, David and Davis, Bob, "Job prospects: Pain from free trade spurs second thoughts; Mr. Blinder's shift spotlights warnings of deeper downside", *Wall Street Journal*, 28 March 2007.

Yenning, "Crackdown on Phumdi Dwellers: An Ugly Face of Developmental Terrorism", *The Sangai Express*, Imphal, Sunday, January 1, 2012.

Index